D0286001

FIRST ENCOUNTER WITH FRANCIS OF ASSISI

DAMIEN VORREUX

TRANSLATED BY
PAUL SCHWARTZ AND PAUL LACHANCE

NEW AND UPDATED EDITION BY
JEAN-FRANÇOIS GODET-CALOGERAS

© Franciscan Institute Publications
St. Bonaventure University
2012

Original edition:
Damien Vorreux, *Première Rencontre avec François d'Assise*
Paris: Les Editions Franciscaines, 1973.

Cover image: The 'Tavola di San Francesco'
200 cms x 100 cms. Painted 1993-1994 by J. G. Holmes
Oil on wood.
'Centro Francescano Internazionale per il Dialogo' Assisi

All rights reserved.
No part of this book may be reproduced or transmitted in any
form or by any means, electronic or mechanical,
without permission in writing from the publisher.

ISBN 13: 978-1-57659-337-0
ISBN 10: 1-57659-337-1
eISBN 13: 978-1-57659-351-6
eISBN 10: 1-57659-351-7

Library of Congress Cataloging-in-Publication Data

Vorreux, Damien
[Première recontre avec François d'Assise. English]
First encounter with Francis of Assisi / Damien Vorreux ; translated by Paul Schwartz and Paul Lachance. -- New and updated ed.
/ by Jean-François Godet-Calogeras.
    p. cm.
Includes bibliographical references (p. 73).
ISBN 978-1-57659-337-0
    1. Francis, of Assisi, Saint, 1182-1226. 2. Christian saints--It-
aly--Assisi--Biography. 3. Assisi (Italy)--Biography. I. Godet-Calogeras, Jean François. II. Title.
    BX4700F6V6413 2012271'.302--dc23
    [B]

                                                  2012010195

Printed in the United States of America
by BookMasters, Inc.
Ashland, Ohio

CONTENTS

Abbreviations Of The Franciscan Sources Used

1C	Thomas of Celano, *The Life of Saint Francis*
1LtCl	Francis's *First Letter to the Clergy*
2C	Thomas of Celano, *The Remembrance of the Desire of a Soul*
2LtCl	Francis's *Second Letter to the Clergy*
2LtF	Francis's *Letter to the Faithful*
2MP	*Mirror of Perfection*
3C	Thomas of Celano, *The Treatise on the Miracles*
AC	*Assisi Compilation*
Adm	Francis's *Admonitions*
DBF	*The Deeds of Saint Francis and his Companions*
ER	*Early Rule* of the Lesser Brothers
FA:ED	*Francis of Assisi: Early Documents*, ed. Regis J. Armstrong, J. A. Wayne Hellmann, William J. Short, 3 volumes (New York: New City Press, 1999-2001)
L3C	*Legend of the Three Companions*
LMj	Bonaventure, *Major Legend of Saint Francis*
LR	*Later Rule* of the Lesser Brothers
LtOrd	Francis's *Letter to the Entire Order*
PrOF	Francis's *Prayer Inspired by the Our Father*
Test	Francis's *Testament*

FOREWORD

First Encounter with Francis of Assisi was first published
in its original French language in 1973. The author, Friar
Damien Vorreux, who died in 1998, began to publish French
translations of the early Franciscan documents in the early
1950s. A couple of decades later, he had certainly become a
savvy translator of those documents, in particular, the writings of Francis of Assisi. When in 1968 the Editions Franciscaines of Paris published the first collection of Franciscan
sources in one volume,[1] his translations took the lion's share
of the book. After those years of companionship with the
Franciscan sources, it is clear that Damien Vorreux was in
a good position to write a very good introduction to the saint
of Assisi, and he did. Almost forty years after its publication
in French, *First Encounter with Francis of Assisi* remains a
book very much worth reading, and that is why the Franciscan Institute Publications have decided to produce a new
edition of it in the English language.

It is my pleasure to bring back some personal memory.
Damien Vorreux and I worked together when, with Théophile
Desbonnets (†1978) and Thaddée Matura, we were preparing
the volume of the writings of Francis of Assisi for the series
"Sources chrétiennes."[2] I was in charge of the French translation of Francis's writings, and we did have some animated
moments since Damien Vorreux and I had a very different
approach to the difficult art of translating. But humor and

---

[1] *Saint François d'Assise: Documents*, Théophile Desbonnets and
Damien Vorreux, eds. (Paris: Editions Franciscaines, 1968).

[2] François d'Assise, *Ecrits*, Théophile Desbonnets, Thaddée Matura,
Jean-François Godet and Damien Vorreux, eds., Sources chrétiennes, 285
(Paris:Editions du Cerf, 1981).

mutual respect always prevailed, and I certainly benefitted more than once from Damien's long experience.

For this new edition of *First Encounter with Francis of Assisi,* the English translation provided in 1979 by Paul Schwartz and Paul Lachance for the Franciscan Herald Press has been totally revisited. The footnotes and the bibliography have been updated and brought to the level of current scholarship. The quotations of the Franciscan early documents have been made according to the current English translation.[3] The translation of the writings of Francis is our own, based on the latest critical edition.[4]

It has been a privilege, and a labor of love and gratitude to prepare this new edition of Damien Vorreux's *First Encounter with Francis of Assisi.*

Jean-François Godet-Calogeras

---

[3] *Francis of Assisi: Early Documents*, Regis J. Armstrong, J. A. Wayne Hellmann and William J. Short, eds., 3 vol. (New York: New City Press, 1999-2001).

[4] Carlo Paolazzi, *Francisci Assisiensis Scripta,* Spicilegium Bonaventurianum, 36 (Grottaferrata: Editiones Collegii S. Bonaventurae, 2009).

PREFACE

"WHY YOU?"

In the thirteenth century the arrival of Saint Francis in the smallest village provoked the enthusiastic and spontaneous outpouring of a kind of popular celebration of the word of God. "Ecco il santo!" "Behold the holy man!" Suddenly bells rang, shops emptied, and street people started milling around. Everyone gathered in the public places to see and hear the "Herald of the Great King." His wandering and preaching took on all the traits of triumphal happenings, all the renewed joy of a Palm Sunday.

A similar excitement can still be felt: literature and the arts, scholarly studies and poems extend the influence of the Poverello; and this man who has been called the Christian Orpheus still works his charms. Even if there is sometimes a snobbish note connected with this, it cannot be denied that Saint Francis enjoys the unanimous praise of artists and theologians, scholars and common folk, nonbelievers or the utterly devout. His name alone evokes admiration and a certain fondness.

Just as spontaneously we find arising in ourselves the question put to him one day by Brother Masseo, a rather dignified friar who was visibly disturbed by these outpourings: "Why you? You are neither handsome, nor learned, nor even noble. Why does everyone run after you?"

"Understand," said Francis, "that God has not found a more vile creature on the earth, and therefore he has chosen me to confound the ... wisdom of the world, so that it may be known that every virtue and every good is from him."[5]

This response is admirable in its simplicity, but it leaves us with our hunger: Even if it is God who acts, we would still like to know how his servant *lets* him act. Grace is common to everyone, but each person uses it in his or her own way.

Why him? Why Francis? Because Francis discovered the secret of how to set the universe into a state of praise and fraternity.

---

[5] DBF 10 (*FA:ED* 3, 583).

I. The Century before the Outbreak

1180-1226: These two dates marking the beginning and end of Francis's life might in themselves seem insignificant, in the real sense of the term. They need only be resituated in their historical context in order to see how a providential mission was prepared and how it later blossomed.

Happy those young people twenty years old in 1220! In every field they were called to become involved in a great and tumultuous adventure of which the chronology published at the end of this book gives only a pale image. Let us look quickly at Christianity in the time of Philip Augustus and Innocent III: We will more easily share their desire for a man sent by God and will welcome this penitent from Assisi with the same fervor.

The Golden Century

In the economic sphere, the West was undergoing its first great increase in trade. Barter was disappearing little by little; trade was king and money attained everyday and universal usage. The crusades unleashed an unprecedented commercial movement; Greeks, Venetians, and Genoans sailed the Mediterranean; goods from both Niger and Scandinavia began to turn up in provincial French towns; Tuscan banks set up exchange branches in important cities like Lyons, Troyes, and as far away as London; they even handled papal finances and took over functions once held by the Curia. Despite repeated condemnations, usury was eating away at the wealth of the aristocracy at the same time that a new class of "haves" began to fill its coffers. The term "usury" in thirteenth-century Florence was only held to apply to loans where the interest was greater than 30 percent! As a new measure of wealth, gold succeeded the square foot of land; it bought comfort, prestige, and power; it opened the doors of political councils, it allowed the purchase of a title, a noble spouse, or an ecclesiastical benefice. Everything was put on the market.

Such was the idol against which Saint Francis would raise the standard of disinterest and holy poverty. These Venetians and Lombards had one passion alone, and it was overriding: doing business. A whole era, an entire civilization, ran the risk of falling headlong into the trap of a dangerous, gilded materialism. One voice had to make itself heard to proclaim once again the necessity of a choice between God and Mammon.[6]

The Century of the Commune

Prosperity was accompanied by a whole series of demographic and political phenomena.

Civilization, heretofore almost exclusively rural, became more urban in a displacement of both population and activity into the city. During the course of the twelfth century, Florence jumped in size from 60 to 187 acres (with a population of 50,000 in 1200); Parma, from 57 to 190; Bologna, from 62 to 247; and Pisa to a total of 30,000 inhabitants in 1228. New city walls and new churches had to be constructed for the *borghi,* and these took on the dimensions of small cities in themselves.

As for the *borghesi,* the "bourgeois" or burghers, they had become a social class that held money, prestige, and power. Because they were involved in all financial and military undertakings, the merchants, bankers, and ship owners gained, if not equality under the law with the nobles, at least an equivalence of privilege, as well as control over the use of

---

[6] Cf. Y. Renouard and B. Guillemain, *Les Hommes d'affaires italiens du moyen âge* (Paris: Tallandier, 2009).

communal finances. They were in control almost everywhere: they elected their own *podestà* and consuls. Occasionally the birth of a commune and accession to political life were accompanied by uprisings, but refractory bishops and lords were eventually swept away by this wave of communalism. It is in this sense that industry and negotiation, having become an essential element of the medieval world, brought to it a veritable revolution, all of whose consequences it would be impossible to list and weigh.[7]

The commune at Assisi was begun in 1200. Francis was twenty years old; he was the son of a very influential fabric merchant. He threw himself with total abandon into the quest for adventure, he experienced the uncontrolled enthusiasm of street demonstrations, he shared in the citywide euphoria at the destruction of the Rocca[8] and the rebuilding of the city's ramparts. His personality would benefit from this liquidation of a collective complex tainted by a rather servile resignation: there is an undeniably "democratic" bent to his thought that already makes him a truly modern man. A trait likewise characteristic of the era is to be found in an examination of the government of the new orders which underwent the same evolution as that of the civil powers. Benedictine administration was typically feudal; the Minors and Preachers would inaugurate a system of elections and the temporary assumption of power at the head of the order and the Provinces.

Urban centralization also created new pastoral needs. There, too, the mendicant orders would adapt themselves, even as far as it concerned their choice of a location for their houses and the style of their preaching. Thanks to them the gospel was brought into the lives of the burghers who, although most open and most influential, were also the most disinherited class religiously and were in danger of falling easy prey to heresy.

---

[7] L. Genicot, *Contours of the Middle Ages* (New York: Barnes & Noble, 1967), 137-38.

[8] The destruction of the Rocca Maggiore fortress which overlooked the city of Assisi took place in 1198 during a conflict between the bourgeoisie of the city and the established nobility.

The Crisis of Monasticism

The ancient Benedictine stock had never been more fruitful and prosperous. The eleventh and twelfth centuries saw the proliferation of monasteries, and vocations and revenues flowed in from all directions. But a spiritual reaction started to take place: Within the cloister itself there was a new tendency to stress asceticism and poverty more than life in common, a life that was also inevitably weighed down by material cares. On the outside, saints like Romuald, Peter Damien, and Jean Gualbert had already put the accent either on a more solitary life or a more effective poverty;[9] Prémontré accelerated this movement which was to become even stronger with Chartreuse, Cîteaux and Grandmont.

It is necessary to keep in mind the spirit of the spiritual offensive occurring both within and on the boundaries of the great orders if we are to situate Saint Francis in his time and appreciate the Franciscan admixture of active and contemplative life, of asceticism and apostolate.

Structure and Heresies

In looking at the diocesan clergy, we must admit that the presence of some cases of greed and immorality were trying the patience of the Christian people. The higher clergy were concerned above all with their material interests: finances and politics. As for the parishes, they were for sale to the highest bidder, leased to priests with no solid training or dignity. Since the spreading of the word of God was no longer assured, others then stepped in to take up the slack. But in what way and at what price!

We thus note the amazing wave of itinerant preachers (Eon of the Star, for instance, or Robert of Arbriselles, or especially the monk Raoul, at once hermit and enlightened dervish) – always ablaze with originality, sometimes with aus-

---

[9] J. Leclercq et al., *The Spirituality of the Middle Ages* (New York: Desclée, 1968), chap. VI.

terity, and occasionally with magic. They ran helter-skelter in an attack on both sin and riches, lords and monks; they unthinkingly overturned structures and consciences, plunging a whole area into a chaos of free-for-all generosity, emotionalism and hallucination, and then went on to stir up even further the good and bad instincts of the crowds.

Scandals on the one side, aspirations more generous than balanced on the other; many, and often the best, were to fall into heresy. There was no shortage of sects waiting for them with open arms. Patarini and Humiliati, Waldensians and Cathars, all cultivated a sense of evangelical poverty, rediscovering the style of the first Christian communities, using the vernacular tongue for prayer or the preaching of a simplified morality and metaphysics, restoring the dignity of manual labor, etc. Francis would espouse these spiritual aspirations of his day – adherence to both the gospel and to poverty – to the extent that some people saw a taint of heresy in him, at least in the beginning. Yet he would never sink into revolt or prideful obstinacy. The boldness of his innovating dynamism was equaled only by his filial submission to the church, which he would reform from within, and to all priests, who were representatives of this church. He would even help the latter to rediscover fidelity to their mission.

Francis realized the impossible task of being the most liberated man in the church of his day and yet the most docile to its hierarchy and its institutions.

Pilgrims and Crusades

The heroic adventure of the pilgrimage had its roots in the discovery of the true cross by Saint Helen in 326. The voyage to Palestine became a social custom. The trip was first made by sea, despite the greed of the Italian ship owners, then later by land, especially following the conversion of Hungary (with the baptism of Saint Stephen in 985). Sanctuaries and hostelries multiplied along every route. This was a fact in the development of civilization which had its importance even in literature, for it would affect the creation of the *chanson de geste* or the medieval verse chronicle.

These mass movements were a phenomenon expressive of a whole mentality. The pilgrim's way of life became like second nature; diverse and often confused motives can be detected there: the penance of voluntary exile, imitating Abraham who consented to leaving his family and native land; the penance also of voluntary submission to the rigors of fatigue and the perils of travel and, for sinners and penitents, of voluntary fasting and self-imposed mortification; the missionary desire to go preach Christ to the pagans; the wish for particular graces; the desire to strengthen one's faith in holy places; and above all the attraction of Jerusalem both as the historically sacred city where Jesus lived, died and was raised, and as the mystical city which was the symbol of the celestial Jerusalem, the goal of our pilgrimage on earth.

It made little difference that this was mixed up with less glorious instincts: "oriental tropism," an elitism fostered (already!) in literature, greed, a commercial sense, the desire for political conquest, etc. The fact is undeniable: This profound cultural event set loose extraordinary movements of masses of people, the reality of which is almost beyond imagination. In 1035 Robert the Magnificent, the Duke of Normandy, set off for the East "with an enormous crowd of people." In 1096 Godfrey of Bouillon led 10,000 knights and 70,000 foot travelers. Around the evening campfires they reminisced that in 1147 Conrad and Louis had led more than 200,000 pilgrims; and they shivered to hear of the troupes of children and faithful whose voyage ended in the slave camps at Alexandria.

"The crusade is an episodic military pilgrimage; the pilgrimage is a continuing popular crusade; the pilgrim is the true Hebrew marching in the desert in search of the Promised Land; the crusader and the pilgrim are the true poor, the real heralds of Jesus Christ." These words of Peter the Hermit and Urban II reverberated in the heads of the Christian people. We will find them taken up again by Saint Francis for himself and for his Friars Minor. This is one aspect – missionary, ascetic and itinerant – of his spirituality which cannot be neglected.[10]

Knights and Troubadours

Every age has its own ideal of humanity, its own image of the hero; in Western literature this image found its expression and its justification as well as its progressive enrichment. Art both mirrors and creates public opinion.

The image of the ideal man at the time of Saint Francis was the courtly knight who was at one and the same time a man of honor, a soldier ready to spill his blood, the lover of an ideal as readily as of a woman, a bit of a stargazer and a candidate for martyrdom who was proud of his muscles, his coat of arms, his charger, and his *Credo*, demonstratively pious and at the same time an outrageous swearer. He was more generous than judicious; but what fearless and· irreproachable faithfulness in the service of our Lord God and of our Lady Mary!

And this image of the knight was spread around in hundreds of stories by the jugglers and troubadours. Epics and cantilenas sounded in everyone's ears, even those considered uncultured. When appropriate, Francis didn't hesitate to begin one of his sermons with a song of courtly love.[11] He would serve poverty as if she were a Lady whose tattered livery he wore. Like Renaud de Montauban, he would rebuild the churches. Surrounded by his first twelve brothers, he compared himself to King Arthur and the Knights of the Round Table. He would cite the achievements of Charlemagne and his paladins.[12] He would even have his own "call to arms": *Pax et bonum!*

---

[10] Cf. P. Alphandéry, *La Chrétienté et l'idée de croisade* (Paris: A. Michel, 1954), and R. Roussel, *Les Pèlerinages à travers les siècles* (Paris: Payot, 1954).

[11] Cf. DBF 9:7: When Saint Francis entered the town, he climbed a wall in order to be more easily heard by the throng, and he preached there to the multitude. In the local idiom this is the theme he set forth: *Tanto è il bene ch'io aspetto / ch'ogni pena m'è diletto* (*FA:ED* 3, 453).

[12] AC 103 (*FA:ED* 2, 208); 2MP 72 (*FA:ED* 3, 320).

But we should not let these picturesque details eclipse the deeply felt attitudes they merely manifest: Saint Francis considered his vocation a dubbing; he was truly the liegeman of the church and its leader, the Lord Pope; he fought on all Christendom's fronts and wanted to shed his blood to push back the boundaries of the Kingdom of God. The *Quest for the Holy Grail* and *Tristan and Iseult* are more than a backdrop or a poetic accompaniment for the life of Saint Francis. These works infected the whole thirteenth century with a fervor and a lifestyle well-represented by the Poverello himself. In his eyes, each of his communities should be at one and the same time both a "court of love" where the highest charity is taught and practiced and a "Round Table" where gallant knights plot their future conquests for the honor of God and. the love of his people.

The Century of Lay People

This quick overview of the pre-Franciscan era would be incomplete if we did not mention an important element which characterizes every field: the progressive accession of lay people to responsibility in the thought, prayer, and action of the church. The clergy's monopoly was broken. Even if everyone who could read or write was called a cleric, outside the clergy the number of those who could think and express themselves increased considerably. We have seen this with the heresies and the communes above.

Writing was more and more for lay people: to satisfy their piety, the books of hours were now directed to the use of the lords or of very rich burghers, rather than to monks alone. The fad for special offices shifted from the cloister, from Cluny above all, to private oratories. Saint Francis himself would compose an Office of the Passion. To clarify the lay person's faith, collections of simple sermons were prepared; the admonitions or sermons of Saint Francis were nothing other than that. The Bible was also translated into ordinary language[13] – or into stone: This was the apogee of Romanesque sculpture and historical bas-reliefs. Not to mention the lives of the saints appearing in prose, we know of over two hundred written in verse. And, finally, it was admitted that lay people could find their salvation outside the cloisters; the Third Orders were founded for them: that of Saint Francis insists less on a rupture with the world than on insertion into it. Tertiaries were associated with the work of spreading the Christian message, and it is significant that here or there they are called *Apostoli* or *Fratres Apostoli*. They were associated with charitable works, particularly with the care of the sick and lepers. Finally, they took part in monastic, parish, or hospital construction, what has been called the "monumental crusade."

Saint Francis appeared at the moment when this delicate shift had to be made: his preaching, which was above all lay preaching with a moral base, disarmed the inflexibility of an obsolete clericalism[14] and reminded everyone that clerics were for the church (and thus for lay people) and not the church for the clerics. While insisting on the rights of Peter against unmandated preachers proclaiming a religion without dogma, he enrolled all people of good will, with no distinction, in the common labor. He mobilized all those, no matter who they were, who were avid for the spirit of God and impatient to serve the church. This was the first great *promotion of the laity* with an awareness of the meaning of vocation and of its mandate.

Did the thirteenth century thus arrive with an atmosphere of the impending end of the world or, on the contrary, with a sense of integral renewal? All values seemed to have

---

[13] A version of Genesis in verse composed around 1190 by Everat for the Countess Marie de Champagne. At the same time the Old and New Testaments were put into verse by Herman of Valenciennes, a task undertaken again in the thirteenth century by John Malkaraume, later by Mace from La-Charité-sur-Loire, etc.

[14] "Over against the old spirit of domination Saint Francis raised and made heard a protest in the name of the Christian ideal.... Without this protest, Christianity would have disappeared from the face of the earth." L. Laberthonnière, "Dieu d'Aristote, dieu de l'Ecole, dieu des chrétiens," *Archivo di Filosofia,* April-June 1933, 32.

been put into question, even the most sacred; social classes either entered into pitched battle or embraced in a great
surge of amity; the frenzy of solitude and renunciation went
side-by-side with the most engaged missionary ardor.

It is like this in all periods of transition that are lived
with great intensity. The thirteenth century was saved from
chaos because the immense crowd seeking nothing but to
have a *total experience of holiness* (always obscurely and often clumsily), at last found its leader, its guide and its model
in Saint Francis. The liturgy sings the radiant apparition,
from a depth deeper than the shadows, of the Franciscan
springtime. And we ourselves, overwhelmed, participate in
this stunning and marvelous resurrection each time we page
through this history that is more beautiful than legend: "Under the gentle hand of this beggar, a heap of gold and luxury
began to bloom like an April hedge."[15]

---

[15] G. Bernanos, "Frère Martin," *Esprit* (October 1951).

II. "I Was Seized by Christ" (Phil 3:12)

The legendary details of Saint Francis's life are familiar to everyone; the *Fioretti* has for quite some time been considered one of the classics of Christianity and it has its place alongside the Bible, the Missal, and the *Imitation of Christ* on family bookshelves. So we won't repeat all those stories here.

Our aim here is to tell how Francis discovered Christ and the gospel, and how his discovery shone out over all the world. Our interest is to better understand the man in order to better understand his accomplishments. To do so we must follow a long route, for Francis would not suddenly become perfect, but he was to pass "gradually from flesh to spirit."[16] For some people, an apparently balanced life is nothing but the sign of a deeper inertia. There are others, however, for whom such balance is the fruit of a continual struggle, one facet of a dynamic tension where opposing forces become reconciled. Francis was one of these exceptional and gifted people.

Umbria and Assisi

Having Umbria for his cradle was his first blessing.[17] Umbria – a land with rolling hills steep enough to produce variety and contrast and to call forth an effort; yet gentle enough

---

[16] 2C 11 (*FA:ED* 2, 250).

[17] "In Umbria one still sees peasants dressed in robes with knotted belts, which was the first outfit of the brothers. The whole countryside reminds one of Saint Francis. It seems that Saint Francis of Assisi could not have been born or have lived anywhere but in Umbria." L. Veuillot,

not to distract eyes looking for contemplation; a permanent invitation to a concrete and rooted prayer. A region where the very air possesses a radiant and almost tangible luminosity, where what is not simple and naive seems to be out of place. A sky whose intense, expansive blue seems so fresh, bringing crickets and hearts to sing. Of all the praises written about Umbria, the most beautiful is undoubtedly the one that compares its springtimes with those of Galilee;[18] more than mere praise, this parallel is a mystery: two countrysides so similar have been able to give the world the Master and his most perfect imitation.

And, on the slope of a little hill, there sits a small city of pink stone: Assisi – a living, even turbulent, town, the opposite of a lazy Romorantine.[19] A town of song and trade, overlooking the road from France to Rome that carries pilgrims and crusaders in rags and fine velvet. A hot-blooded town where talk about taking up arms against Perugia heats up every couple of months. A town where money, politics, and religion (three absolutes then inseparable) are all the topic of conversation; where the bishop and the podestà square off for a fight amid great shouts before being reconciled amid crocodile tears: sincerely, but only for a short time. A commune where all the inhabitants fraternize in the cool breeze of the evening on the piazza with an easy-going familiarity. There is nothing like a modern city here, that "bourgeois shop, a silo full of tenants, barrel upon barrel of human sauerkraut." (Paul Claudel!).[20] Renan, that master craftsman, de-

---

Carnet de voyage, 1874, cited by E. Veuillot, *Louis Veuillot,* vol. IV (Paris: Lethielleux, 1913), 494

[18] E. Renan, *Lettre à Berthelot,* May 11, 1850 (Rome: Forzani, 1888).

[19] Editor's note: Romorantin is an archetypical French provincial city, off the beaten path and known for its wine produced from grapes of the same name. Used here it indicates the opposite of the bustling Assisi.

[20] P. Claudel, *Conversations dans le Loir-et-Cher* (Paris: Gallimard, 1935), 143.

clared: "Florence seems like a Boeotia[21] to me ever since I've seen Assisi."[22]

This was the backdrop for Francis's first twenty years. A happy country, a happy temperament. Blessings such as these pointed toward really harsh demands. But the gentle mercy of the Lord does not stop there.

Milord Bernardone and Lady Pica

Did Francis's father have a great moral influence on his son? When he appears on the historical scene, he behaves in an unfortunate way and with a surly disposition that cannot be taken as a sign of a very elevated spirituality.[23] He was a red-faced blusterer, a rich fabric merchant, very tight with his ducats; at the same time he was also a courageous man who crossed the Alps at least twice a year and who had no fear of highwaymen when he left for the fairgrounds of Champagne to stock up on material. He was rich and determined to appear so, not uninterested in the quite original publicity generated by his eldest son's fantasies in food, drink, and extravagant clothing.[24] He was, moreover, proud of his son, of the noble education he had given him, of his youthful pranks at which he laughed loudest. To his credit, we should note that he was a man of taste and some class, since he chose Dame Pica as his bride.

French and noble, Pica was of the house of Bourlémont.[25] She was a gentle and silent spirit whom Celano compared to Saint Elizabeth, mother of the Precursor.[26] With what faith

---

[21] Boeotia is a central region of Greece known for its military importance and ease of communication but whose inhabitants were generally considered to be dull.

[22] Cf. also another "craftsman": A. Suares, *Sienne la bien-aimée* (Paris: Emile-Pa, 1932), chapters 5 and 6.

[23] 1C 12-14 (*FA:ED* 1, 191-93).

[24] L3C 2 (*FA:ED* 2, 68-69).

[25] Cf. C. Frassen, *La Règle du Tiers-Ordre de la Pénitence* (Paris: E. Couterot, 1683), 272.

[26] 2C 3 (*FA:ED* 2, 241-43).

and sensitivity she must have used the educational methods of the time!

She took the little child by the hand and led him as if on pilgrimage to the baptistery of Saint Rufino where, christened John, he became a son of God; she recounted sacred history while commenting on the sculptures of the parish church; she tutored him in between two courses given by the priest at Saint George: Their two foreheads bent over a great psalter (the only textbook then in use) where Francis was introduced to religious lyricism at the same time as his alphabet. The text he assimilated so well that he could later compose out of free-standing verse the finely structured psalms of his Office of the Passion. In the evening next to the hearth she told him stories of knightly deeds or sang him one of those exquisite needlework songs which since the twelfth century had already become "songs of yesteryear," cantilenas of his native province. Also, in the same way that "Francis" became the real forename of the saint, so French would become his true mother tongue, the one he would spontaneously rediscover whenever impetuous feelings of joy or compassion invaded his soul.[27]

As mistress of the house, her orders were already thank-yous, her activity a smile, her hospitality a due. Firm when it was necessary, she dared to reopen the grill on the dungeon where Bernardone had thrown Francis for his crime of conversion.[28] She was one of those mothers whose Christian reflections on various events have the resonance of a *Magnificat*; whose prayer kept unceasing watch on the growth of Christ in the soul of her little one; a mother whom her son would easily imagine seated next to the crèche or standing at the foot of the cross.

Captivity: A Year's Retreat

Twenty years passed like an enchantment, in the euphoria of sun and good health, of music and friendship: twenty

---

[27] Cf. 1C 16 (*FA:ED* 1, 194-95); 2C 13 and 127 (*FA:ED* 2, 252 and 331).
[28] 1C 13 (*FA:ED* 1, 192-93).

years of happiness and harmonious formation. At the age when so many choices come forward to claim a whole life, God presented him not with the ideal young woman of which he undoubtedly often dreamt, but with a fiancée austere as well as radiant, whose liegeman he would be up until his death: the cross.

Armies were being raised against Perugia. The young patrician saw here an unhoped-for opportunity for a full life. To the devil with this fabric business! He had no doubt about his vocation: It was knighthood with its train of glory, the intoxication of blows struck and taken, the tales of courage "which will be spoken of in ladies' chambers," the riches of booty, and who-knows-what-else ..., perhaps the granting of a noble title and being dubbed on the battlefield. Pica and Bernardone, having spared no expense to furnish him with trappings, horses, and valets, watched him go with tears of pride; they shared the same dream of greatness, without wondering to themselves whether God wasn't leading their son to a far more beautiful epic journey.

Francis left Assisi thus, one of the more lively of his group, his lips full of nothing but words of victory and triumphal return. Alas! With all his company he was surrounded near Saint John's bridge, conquered, and taken prisoner. His jailers were rough: overcrowding, promiscuity, cold and hunger, waiting and incertitude – circumstances where men reveal themselves. *Francis sang.* Not that he was less sensitive than his friends to their misery: As a spoiled child suddenly tossed behind bars, he must have undergone a violent shock. But he repulsed the insidious temptations of discouragement and degradation; instead of turning in upon his own regret he deliberately opted for attention to those around him. And his whole repertoire of songs of love or battle helped to distract, perhaps to cheer up, his coprisoners who were chomping at the bit. This was at once the expression and the safeguard of his great heart.

A forced retreat, but what a retreat! One year of reflection necessarily distills a philosophy, if not a mystique, in a person's soul; one year of self-abandonment under conditions more nearly favorable to unbridled egoism was his first step upon a path that would always remain a path of generosity. His conversion, like every other, started thus: "The hand of the Lord was upon him and Francis little by little saw his inner world transformed."[29]

Among the Lepers: A Hard Novitiate

Why shouldn't the outside world also have changed for him? After being released he returned home with a new spirit, with new eyes. He found his beautiful *Umbria verde* once again, but "the beauty of the fields, the cheerful aspect of the vines and the woods, had all lost its charm."[30] He found his friends and their banquets once again, but their noisy company weighed upon him from then on; he abandoned the carefree gangs which were now too vulgar and superficial for him. He came back to trade and business once again, but he had lost all interest in these activities and found no sense there. He wanted to try his hand at military life once again, feeling strongly that his whole life should be a giving of himself without reserve. He left to rejoin Gautier of Brienne, commander of the pontifical militia, but at Spoleto a voice broke into his sleep with a dialogue worthy of the road to Damascus:

> "Francis, where are you going?"
> "To fight in Pouille!"
> "From whom do you expect more, from the master or from the servant?"
> "From the master."
> "Then why follow the servant?"
> "Lord, what do you want me to do?"
> "Go back to your country: there your calling will be shown to you..."

---

[29] 1C 2-3 (*FA:ED* 1, 183-85).
[30] 1C 3 (*FA:ED* 1, 184-85).

With this farewell to war, a more demanding campaign began, one he later summed up in these words: "When I was still in sin the sight of lepers disgusted me; but the Lord led me among them and I did mercy with them."[31] In fact, one day as he rode through the countryside he met one of these unfortunates on the road. Once his first reaction of repulsion had passed, he took the leper in his arms and kissed him. This was a new discovery of Christ and a new approach to the Cross.

There he was caught in love's trap. The next day he returned to the Holy Savior sick-house,[32] gave alms to each of the entombed residents, and with his lips placed a kiss on every sore. Then he spent some time among those whom he would henceforth refer to only as "my brothers in Christ" or "my Christian brothers."[33] This was the mystery of Christ suffering in his members; the mystery that the faithful of the middle ages rediscovered at every moment, whether in the liturgical readings of the Servant Songs: "We considered him a leper,"[34] in the many sculptures or stained glass windows showing Christ as a suffering leper, or even in the legends of some monks who, believing they were carrying a leper on their shoulders, discovered that they carried Christ himself in person. This was the mystery with which the young Francis became especially familiar over the long period he spent with the Crucigere brothers (literally: "the cross-bearers") who ran the Holy Savior hospital, as well as with the infirmarians of Saint Anthony who ran a leprosarium in Rome[35] where he spent some time in 1210. The latter group displayed as their distinctive emblem the famous Tau (T) that Francis would later adopt as the sign of his order.

---

[31] Test 2 (*FA:ED* 1, 124).

[32] Halfway between Assisi and Saint Mary of the Angels, on the present site of Casa Gualdi.

[33] 2MP 58 (*FA:ED* 3, 303).

[34] Isaiah 53:4.

[35] Cf. O. van Rieden, *Das Leiden Christi im Leben des hl. Franziskus von Assisi* (Rome: Istituto Storico Cappuccini, 1960), 15-16. On the Antonines or Hospital Brothers of St. Anthony, see the article in the *New Catholic Encyclopedia*.

The "Go!" That Creates Prophets

His vocation was becoming clearer, but the deciding event
would take place at San Damiano. Here was a stage well set
for such a scene: a cloistered calm, an orchard truly set for an
annunciation scene with an old curé limping about, mixing
his psalms with the songs of birds in the trees, and a little
dilapidated chapel with a meditative and taciturn façade
and a simple rose window of stone. Waiting for him over the
altar was a great Byzantine Christ that Francis particularly
liked because it represented a redeemer at once friendly and
triumphant. This savior did not seem to say to the faithful,
"Look how I suffered for you!" but "Look how much I love
you!" It was "a Christ of peace and persuasion."[36]

And this is exactly what Francis needed. He entered the
chapel with the slow and shuffling steps of the neophyte who
has already experienced an inner conversion, but who has
of yet no sure idea where to apply his external activity. He
prostrated himself before the cross in order to finally receive
some light. His prayer has been saved for us: "Most high and
glorious God, come and enlighten the shadows of my heart;
give me a right faith, a solid hope, and a perfect love, as well
as a sense of the godly and the clear sight necessary to accom-
plish your holy will that will never lead me astray. Amen."

From the crucifix at that moment rang out the same voice
that called Abraham, Moses, the prophets, and the apostles,
the voice that sets its chosen one apart, calls him by his
name, and confirms him in God's service:

"Francis, go repair my house which is falling into ruin!"

And he, feeling nothing but availability and service,
unhesitatingly applied this order to the little tumbledown
sanctuary: he became a mason. Only later did he realize that
his mission really concerned the "living church that Christ
bought with his blood."[37] For the moment, he consecrated

---

[36] Paul Sabatier, *Etudes inédites sur saint François d'Assise* (Paris: Fischbacher, 1932), 167.

[37] 2C 11 (*FA:ED* 2, 249-50).

himself solely to the restoration of these stone walls: One after the other, San Damiano, San Pietro, and Saint Mary of the Angels all felt the work of his mallet; he was busy with his trowel. He wanted no more than to take his place among the thousands of penitents of his day who shared between themselves the service of the sick and lepers, pilgrimages, the giving of alms, and the building of churches.

But the "go!" was heard; the spirit had been kindled; the Franciscan movement would never stop again.

"Leave Your Home!"

A break with the world. But not without some heartbreak. The gospel affirms: "He who loves his father more than me is not worthy of me." Francis was called upon to make a choice.

To finance his restoration of the churches, Francis one day took "several pieces of fabric" from his father's shop, galloped off to Foligno, sold his goods, and even – what luck! – found a buyer for his horse. Then he returned to Assisi, respectfully entered the church whose repair he felt it his mission to undertake, went to find the priest in charge (who was very poor), offered him the money for its repair, and requested permission to stay with the priest for a while. Agreeing to this request, the priest refused the money out of fear of Francis's family.

> Bernardone, the fleshly father of a son of grace, then hauled him before the bishop for Francis to renounce all his rights of inheritance. The latter willingly presented himself before the bishop's tribunal and, not waiting a moment or hesitating the least bit, without waiting for an order or an explanation, quickly took off all his clothes and gave them to his father. In his admirable fervor brought on by his spiritual drunkenness, he declared before the assembly: 'Until now I called you my father on earth. From now on I can say with assurance: Our Father who is in heaven ...' The

bishop had him given the homespun cloak of one of his tenants; Francis received it with acknowledgment and, picking up a piece of chalk from the road, traced a large cross upon it.[38]

A Reading of the Gospel

Two years were spent in this "state of penance" where hospitals, the roads, masonry, begging, and meditation played such a great role. And then, one beautiful morning on the 24th of February, a new illumination occurred.

Francis was participating in the mass of Saint Mathias. "Then the moment for the gospel came. The clumsy priest noisily turned the page, made an enormous sign of the cross, and in his most officious voice began: 'Go and proclaim everywhere that the kingdom of heaven is at hand. Take neither gold nor silver, nor a purse for your route, nor two tunics, nor sandals, nor a staff ...'" Francis started. Here were honest, everyday words, perfectly familiar, neutral, inert, pure clichés. Ages ago they had been tamed, stripped of beak and claw, taught to roll over and play dead: real word-mummies. But this morning they seemed strangely new and pure, compact, stocky, literally unforgettable. This morning the words *made sense.* This sleeping gospel suddenly awoke. Francis wanted to seize its uncluttered heart. Right after the *Ite missa est,* he asked the priest, "Hasn't anyone read that? Read it word-to-word and body-to-body, like a love letter, like an order from the admiralty?"[39]

The old priest went over the text with him point by point, and Francis, ecstatic with joy, drunk with the Holy Spirit, said: "This is what I want, *this is what I've been looking for!*" Then and there he undid his sandals, threw away his staff, replaced his belt with a length of rope, made up a habit in the shape of a cross, and, certain from then on of his calling, set out to preach the gospel around the world to every creature.

---

[38] LMj 2:1-3 (*FA:ED* 2, 536-38).

[39] J. Delteil, *François d'Assise* (Paris: Flammarion, 1960), 72-75.

He gave his first sermon in the church of Saint George where he had learned to read.[40]

In a Christendom in a State of Council

Living and preaching the gospel, some months later there were twelve of them sharing this ideal. Bernard of Quintavalle was the first to come; Giles and Sylvester followed, then Juniper and Leo, Philip and Peter, Angelo and Masseo, Leonard and John ...

Their project was to be neither hermits nor monks; it was what all their contemporaries called "apostolic life," a life alternately divided between prayer and the work of preaching or charitable activity. Their first foothold, Rivo Torto, for instance, designated by the least pretentious term possible, *luoghi* – "places" and not convents – was only intended for use during the contemplative or communitarian periods of this "apostolic life." They were places of prayer and recovery following work and episodic dispersion; at the same time they were places of fraternal living and of eremitic life lived in fraternity. As for active life and work, there was no house: just the road and the stars above. Meals and sometimes lodging were taken where they worked or in the hospitals in exchange for their varied services.

But they wanted to realize this ideal *within the church.* This is why twelve "penitents from Assisi" – the name they gave themselves – presented themselves before Pope Innocent III in 1210. This was a step radically distinct from those taken by the heretics of that time, who willingly brandished the gospel against the church. Like them, Francis wanted to reform the church; but it is from the church alone that he desired both his mandate and the needed grace. And these he obtained, in spite of Curial hesitation, thanks to the intervention of Cardinal John Colonna, who observed: "If we reject the rule of this poor man as impractical, don't we at the same time affirm that the gospel is impractical?" Innocent III

---

[40] 1C 21-22 (*FA:ED* 1, 201-02).

welcomed the brothers and gave them his approbation, with the authorization to "preach penance" in short exhortations.

Five years later, he convoked the Fourth Lateran Council. Francis, at that point the head of a family of nearly 5,000 brothers, found himself there in the capacity of an observer[41] to receive the instructions of their common Father. The opening sermon of the council was a sensation throughout Christendom and sounded like a trumpet blast announcing a general reform. Francis was deeply touched by this; all his later works were influenced. Commenting on a text from the prophet Ezekiel, Innocent III called upon the participants to mark themselves and all Christians with the Tau of penance and of the cross:

> "Tau is the last letter of the Hebrew alphabet and its shape designates a cross, at least before the fixing of Pilate's proclamation. Such is the sign one bears on one's head if one manifests the radiance of the cross in all one's behavior; if, as the apostle says, one crucifies one's flesh with its vices and sins, and if one affirms: I do not desire to put my glory in anything but the cross of our Lord Jesus Christ through whom the world has been crucified for me and me for the world.... Be, then, champions of the Tau and of the cross!"

And after recalling that God does not will the death of a sinner but his conversion, he ordered them to preach penance and forgiveness everywhere.

At this point Francis chose the Tau as the symbol of his penitential life and as the résumé of his preaching: as the concrete emblem of the participation of his order in the reform of the church and of souls. The Tau would serve him as a signature for his letters and as a standard up until the day

---

[41] In addition, moreover, to Saint Dominic, for the Council discussed, among other things, the recognition of new orders. Cf. Father Cuthbert, O.S.F.C., *Life of Saint Francis of Assisi* (New York: Longmans, Green & Co., 1948), 213 ff.

when the stigmata would reproduce in his very flesh the content of this mystical letter imprinted in his heart.

"The Jugglers of God"

Preach the gospel, certainly. But *live* it first of all. How did they live in these new fraternities?

What was essential was not to be found in their behavior or outward activities, but in their inner attitude. A Lesser Brother defined himself not by external activity but by his internal attitude. He was not asked "What do you do?" but "Who are you?" And he should respond in terms of the beatitudes before speaking of his work, ministry, or apostolate. Grossly oversimplifying, we can say in pedantic terms that the *vis a tergo,* the internal dynamism and secret of the united fraternities, was more important than the *vis ab ante,* the clear idea that brings about the coherence of organized groups capable of intense productivity.

Living the gospel in fraternities: such was the ideal at Rivo Torto and at the Portiuncula; to so love Christ that one could not help but see him everywhere and imitate him in everything. Obedience, poverty, and chastity are seen as an alignment with Christ and are willed in reference to Christ: they are *religious acts* even before they are personal asceticism, the means of communal discipline, or a method of influence. And all this in fraternity, for

> if a mother nourishes and cherishes her son of the flesh, with how much more affection should each one nourish and cherish his brother in the spirit![42]

The applications of this beautiful plan varied to no end. Office and prayer alternated with diverse sorts of labor. While some set off for long-term missions, others retired into solitude, three or four together, in a hermitage in the Rieti valley. All of them, despite their differences in temperament,

---

[42] LR 6 (*FA:ED* 1, 103).

displayed an unmistakable family sentiment, one of whose traits was a joyful familiarity, at once courtly and comradely, that led them to rely more on poetry, music, and dramatization than upon dialectic and artifice. In their frank simplicity, a *Canticle of the Sun* and a crèche at Greccio seemed more efficacious than scholarly theses in giving the common people a grasp of God.

The time had long passed when they had been taken for fools. Jeerers started to wonder, cowards no longer pelted them with stones. Soon all Italy had been won over. The recruitment curve climbed almost to the vertical.

The Spread of the Order

The golden century worked a veritable run on poverty: around 1220 the order comprised almost 10,000 brothers and the success of these mendicants submitted to the church constituted the best antidote to heresy in the West. For women, too, fraternities had to be founded: Saint Clare of Assisi was the first of the Poor Ladies (from her comes the name Poor Clares, by which they are known today). As for married people hungry for the gospel, the Third Order would give them, through profession, a way to lead a consecrated life without abandoning their status: Saint Francis wrote his *Letter to the Faithful* for them, and it was the starting point of their rule.

Geographical expansion followed too: One after another, France, England, Germany, Hungary, and Spain saw these strange, poor preachers and wanderers arrive. And, finally, there was also social expansion: The Tau crusade was extended to all classes, nobles and laborers, the ignorant and the learned. Yet, due to the massive entry of students and professors, the order little by little became clericalized. The social and intellectual range of the new recruits was enriching, but also posed risks as much for fraternal life as for the interpretation of the primitive ideal. The order faced its first crisis which had a sad result in the soul of the Poverello.

With increasing numbers, in effect, came the threat of deviation and weakening of purpose. There were those, said Brother Giles, "who entered religion with no change whatever in their lifestyle; they are like the laborer who took up the arms of Roland but knew neither how to fight nor how to joust with them."[43] The best intentions often lead to the worst deviations, especially when ruthlessness is combined with the conviction that one is defending the best interests of the church. All claimed they were of Francis, yet here and there could be felt the wind of an intolerant exclusivity that was hardly Franciscan. Two tendencies within the movement dug in their heels: some swore only by manual work and the care of lepers; others submitted all to the intellectual demands of the proclamation of the word of God. The former wanted no book other than the crucifix; the latter took pains to show that a well-stocked library was an instrument of labor conceded and even required by the rule. Some assisted at office in the parishes, others wanted their own conventual church packed with the faithful from neighboring parishes. Some called upon poverty to justify their wood and thatched huts, others called upon the same poverty to justify their stone houses, ability to resist both rain and fire. The most rigid held to begging only for something to eat and to wear, fearing contact with money like the plague, while others more prudent wanted to create a "revolving fund" able to assure the strict necessities and to underwrite needs other than food, like buildings, books, sacred vessels, etc.

Even though the beginnings had been marked by such a beautiful diversity, a real source of riches, Satan came to stir up the waters in order to make his catch, and diversity sometimes became division. Francis had to struggle against his naive confidence in spontaneous generosity; he had to resolve to legislate, to somehow put the gospel in the terms of the chancellery. He had the tragic impression, rereading certain sections of the rule, of having put parapets where there should have been stepping-stones, of having exhausted him-

---

[43] *Sayings of Brother Giles* 16, in *Golden Words: The Sayings of Brother Giles of Assisi* (Chicago: Franciscan Herald Press, 1990).

self conjuring up cowardice when he would have preferred opening up avenues to the Holy Spirit and to fervor.

The problems troubling the order thus also tormented its founder in a personal way. Two deep reflexes would save him from despair: First, a reflex of submission to the church. He knew that it was she, after all, that founds orders by giving them more than a *nihil obstat,* by conferring upon them their efficacy of grace and of salvation. He thus allowed her to organize into a more structured society the numerous sons he entrusted to her, and she in fact proceeded with infinitely more tact and gentleness than is often admitted. Cardinal Hugolino, who helped Francis in the final redaction of the rule of life, was a friend and admirer of Francis. If the successive versions of the rule would manifest a more and more juridical air, its heart would nonetheless be safe: How could Christ have been deleted, by his spouse, from the life of his sons?

The second reflex was one of transcending conflict by a spurt of personal generosity. The Spirituals wanted above all to be a reproach to their brothers; he wanted to be no more than an example. The formalists risked falling into the idolatry of one text of the rule; he wanted to be the always more present, living, and responding incarnation of the ideal he envisioned and proposed. The more the ideal became letter, the more the head of the line should become spirit and life. This requirement brought to still more pointed development in Francis the desire to become like Christ in all things, including even martyrdom. This would lead him to sainthood, by way of the stigmata.[44]

---

[44] The severity of the crisis, the mystery of the setback, and the long journey toward the peace of God are presented with a rare sensitivity and much insight by E. Leclerc in his two works: *The Wisdom of the Poverello* (Chicago: Franciscan Herald Press, 1961) and *Exile and Tenderness* (Chicago: Franciscan Herald Press, 1965).

A Sense of the Human

Balance is a term that is well applied to the Poverello in spite of everything. A champion of going beyond oneself, sometimes of immoderation, he nonetheless remains so human that our memory of him has been able to survive the stereotypes of hagiography which would have condemned him to remain fixed and frozen in stained glass. Just the opposite has happened, in fact; we really would not be surprised to see him walking once again on our roads, praying at our side, eating at our table, settling his fraternal look on us and on every living creature.

We will encounter other revealing details later; but there are some which we cannot pass over here:

— The joy for which he gave such vibrant praise.[45]

— The sensitivity toward a young brother who overestimated his own resistance during Lent; Francis broke his own fast and had a meal served to the whole community to save the novice from the shame of eating alone.[46]

— The big smile accompanying the multiplication of provisions in the middle of the sea for the crew which took him on board at no charge.[47]

— The flash of roguishness in his eyes while telling a guide dying of thirst in the mountains, "Go look behind this rock!" Like a new Moses, he made water spring from the stone.[48]

— The hearty humor where we rediscover all the medieval universe in his duels with the demon: either when, tempted by luxury, he made a row of snowmen and said, "There are your wife and children; now go get them food and clothing, for they are cold!"[49]; or when he advised Brother Rufino to chase away a demon with a lively exorcism: "Open your mouth so I can urinate inside!"[50]

---

[45] 2C 125 and 128 (*FA:ED* 2, 329-31).

[46] AC 50 (*FA:ED* 2, 149-50).

[47] 1C 55 (*FA:ED* 1, 229-30).

[48] 2C 46 (*FA:ED* 2, 278).

[49] 2C 117 (*FA:ED* 2, 325).

[50] DBF 33 (*FA:ED* 3, 617-20).

– The sense of earthly realities: Knowing that we catch more flies with one spoonful of honey than with a barrel of vinegar, he ordered good wine and cheese served to "our brother brigands."[51]

– The gentle irony toward a squad of soldiers whose every attempt at reprovisioning had failed: "But, of course, you have been trying to buy things. Go out and beg, then come back and tell me what happened." They did so; and their daily ration had never been so delicious and copious.[52]

– And, finally, his exquisite poetry. But here it would be necessary to devote pages to recall all the stories about animals, each one better than the last: the conversion of the wolf of Gubbio,[53] the silence imposed for a while on some sparrows who were disturbing a sermon,[54] the punishing of a mean sow that had killed a lamb,[55] and what is undoubtedly the most beautiful: the sermon to the birds.[56]

Our Brother Saracens

It remains to examine one last aspect of his religious personality and of his vocation: his mission to the unbelievers.

July 16, 1212, marked the victory of Las Navas of Tolosa. All of Europe was awash in a wave of enthusiasm. In Francis's spirit this event would crystallize around one single adventure many supernatural force that were always seeking new expression: the desire to conquer for Christ the souls saved by his blood especially those most disinherited; obedience to the Church which was relaunching the Crusade in all its forms; and, finally, a desire for martyrdom. He cried out,

The emperor Charles, Roland, Olivier, all the knights and gallant warriors who were mighty in combat

---

[51] AC 115 (*FA:ED* 2, 221-22).
[52] 2C 77 (*FA:ED* 2, 297-98).
[53] DBF 23 (*FA:ED* 3, 482-85).
[54] 1C 59 (*FA:ED* 1, 235).
[55] 2C 111 (*FA:ED* 2, 321).
[56] 1C 58 (*FA:ED* 1, 234).

pursued the infidels to their death, avoiding neither
sweat nor fatigue; and to finish this, these holy martyrs died fighting for the faith of Christ. And we want
to reap glory and honor by contenting ourselves with
singing their exploits![57]

Francis venerated these crusaders who died in combat like
martyrs. He also would go to seek death among the nonbelievers but fighting only to bring them the faith.

The sixth year after his conversion [thus, 1212], afire
with a desire for martyrdom, he resolved to go to
Syria to preach the Christian faith to the Saracens.
He set out by ship, but the winds were against them;
he found himself washed up on the coast of Slavonia,
then returned to Ancona.[58]

The first missionary expedition was short-lived.
Not missing a step, he took off once again, this time attempting the land route to Morocco by way of Spain.

So strong was his desire for martyrdom that the saint
sometimes outdistanced his traveling companion,
Bernard of Quintavalle, and ran, drunk with the spirit, to the realization of his great project.[59]

He followed the provincial route of Saint James of Compostella, very probably met Saint Dominic at Perpignan,[60] and
went at least as far as Vitoria in Spain where, faithful still to
the traditions of the origins, he repaired a chapel dedicated
to Saint Mary Magdalene.[61] But he fell gravely ill and had to
return to Italy a second time.

---

[57] AC 103 (*FA:ED* 2, 209).

[58] 1C 55 (*FA:ED* 1, 229-30). Slavonia was the medieval name of Dal-
matia.

[59] 1C 56 (*FA:ED* 1, 230).

[60] J. Tolra de Bordas, *L'Ordre de saint François d'Assise en Roussillon*
(Paris: V. Palmé, 1884), 1-19.

[61] Cf. *Acta Sanctorum* vol. 50, 699 d, confirmed by local tradition. Remains of that sanctuary disappeared totally in 1945.

He had to wait until 1219 to finally realize his plan. Along with brothers Peter, Illuminatus, and Leonard he went aboard a troop transport carrying reinforcements to Damietta. When he presented himself at the Saracen camp he underwent all kinds of ill treatment, but with what happiness! And yet, because he kept crying, "Sultan! Sultan!" he wound up being led to the tent of the Sultan Al-Malik who received him courteously. The conviction of his faith, his inspired attitudes, and his scorn of wealth and death made a deep impression on Al-Malik. He was not converted, but provided safe passage and the possibility of preaching the faith and of going on to the Holy Land.[62]

No conversion of unbelievers, no martyrdom: a complete failure. But God kept to himself the right to authenticate this perfect copy of his crucified son by another kind of martyrdom.

The stigmata

To really understand this event, and even before retracing the historical circumstances, it is good to recall that there exists in mysticism a phenomenon – interior and sometimes exterior – well-known to theologians, described and catalogued under the somewhat vague label of "the wound of mystical love."[63] To the extent that the love of God grows in a person, the latter better understands who God is and who he is himself; God appears at once more and more desirable and more and more inaccessible. How can one realize a union, the desire of which becomes so vehement and saddening, if not by loving God as his own son loved him, by "taking on oneself in love the sufferings of his son"?[64]

---

[62] For a thorough and recent study of the crusades, Islam and Francis' mission of peace, see P. Moses, *The Saint and the Sultan* (New York: Doubleday Religion, 2009).

[63] Cf. citations of St. John of the Cross in: J. Lebreton, *Tu Solus Sanctus, Etudes de théologie mystique* (Paris: Beauchesne, 1948); A. Cabassut, "Blessure d'amour" in *Dictionnaire de Spiritualité* X, 1724-79.

[64] St. Paul of the Cross, *Lettere,* vol. III, 149.

Celano sees correctly when he places the first (wholly interior) act of the stigmatization back at the dialogue with the crucifix of San Damiano: "From this moment on, compassion for the crucified one was anchored in his spirit; from this moment, too, the stigmata of the passion were imprinted very deeply in his heart before appearing in his flesh."[65] For eighteen years "the cross of Christ took the place of a book for him; day and night he recalled its mystery to himself."[66] He was in a permanent state of stigmatization.

In autumn of 1224, Francis decided to observe the fast of Michaelmas in the hermitage of La Verna. Thanks to Brother Leo who was spying, we have the text of two prayers that he repeated to satiety: "Lord, who are you and who am I?" and "Lord, allow me to feel in my body and in my soul the sufferings of your passion; allow me to feel in my heart the love with which you burn and which brought you to suffer so much hurt for us sinners!"[67]

Suddenly he sensed the request answered: a crucified man on six fiery wings appeared in the heavens; Francis's heart was stupified, full of superhuman joy and heartrending compassion. When the vision disappeared, he noted the extraordinary miracle: His hands and feet had been pierced by nails, his open side was bleeding profusely; body and soul he had become like Christ. He could say with Saint Paul: "We who possess the spirit of the Lord and his freedom, we can with an open face reflect as in a glass the glory of the Lord, for we are changed into the same image: Such is the action in us of the Lord who is Spirit."[68]

Immediately following his stigmatization, Francis composed what we can call his *Magnificat:* He wrote with his own pierced hand.[69] It is an explosion of joy, a litany to the praise of "the merciful Savior." There is no allusion to the exceptional grace he had just received other than his signature

[65] 2C 10 (*FA:ED* 2, 249).

[66] LMj 4:3 (*FA:ED* 2, 551).

[67] DBF 9 (*FA:ED* 3, 452-58).

[68] 2 Corinthians 3:17-18.

[69] The original is still to be found at the Sacro Convento in Assisi.

on the back: the famous letter Tau, his real *labarum,* always
a sign of crusade and of victory.

Some days later he left La Verna without forgetting
– saints also have manners – to thank and bid farewell to
"brother falcon" who woke him for matins every night. He
knew that this time the farewell would be final.

Death

The voyage from La Verna to Assisi was both a triumph
and a Way of the Cross. News of the miracle spread wide
and quick. Each village gave him a delerious welcome and
pressed him to stay with them in the hope that he would
work miraculous cures for them. Città di Castello managed
to get him to stay one month.

He traveled on a donkey, crossing the Apennines through
heavy snows. He was losing blood from all his wounds and
a heavy veil spread across his tired eyes, so burned by the
eastern sun and by constant weeping. His body grew weaker,
sapped by his fasting. Despite all this, he continued his life
as a pilgrim-preacher to the end: every step was a pretext for
another sermon. What more convincing proclamation of the
gospel could he make than preaching it through the evidence
of his martyrdom, his prayer, and his obstinate zeal?

The itinerary passed through Cortona, Gubbio, and Noc-
era in order to avoid Perugia which coveted his mortal remains. Assisi was loudly proclaiming its rights to any future
relics and sent out an armed escort to meet his party, guard-
ing against any kidnapping.

Francis came to San Damiano at the end of his rope.
Saint Clare moved him into a small hut covered by matted
branches at the bottom of the garden. In the night, small field
mice scurried across his body. And this pitiable blind man, in
agony, composed the masterpiece of the bright and lyrical literature of all time: the *Canticle of the Sun.* The world for him
was no longer hostile, but fraternal; not opaque, but luminous. Francis once again found a joyful peace with creation

and with himself because he was in peace, in total conformity with God.

The stigmatized man who, in Paul Claudel's beautiful phrase, "was with Christ no more than a suffering and redemptive thing," remained truly human and truly poor until the end. Nothing was more touching than the humility with which he expressed the needs and wants of his illness. Only a Pharisee could be scandalized by the last desires of this agonizing man: parsley, frangipani, and music. The parsley was miraculously discovered in the garden by a reluctant brother who came upon it despite the night's darkness.[70] The almond frangipani was brought – along with his shroud – by "brother Jacqueline" for whom there was no enclosure.[71] And an angel came and played relaxing and refreshing music at the head of the dying man's bed.[72]

His mission was completed. He dictated his *Testament* to leave behind him in writing the last and most perfect expression of his ideal. Then he himself decided how he would spend the last moments of his life. How many times had he not taught that the Friars Minor were "true Israelites crossing the desert of this world like pilgrims and strangers, and that they should unceasingly celebrate with the soul of a poor man the Lord's Passover, that is, his passage from this world to that of the Father"![73] This is why he modeled his death on the last days of Christ.

Carried to Mary of the Angels, he had himself laid out naked on the naked earth and only accepted the garments his guardian offered him with the understanding that they were on loan. He asked for some bread and, like Christ on Holy Thursday, blessed it and gave it to his brothers. He had the Passion according to Saint John read; hearing it, his brothers applied it both to Christ and to his stigmatized servant, stretched out on the earth before their eyes: "One would have said that he had just been taken down from the

---

[70] 2C 51 (*FA:ED* 2, 281).
[71] 3C 38 (*FA:ED* 2, 418).
[72] 2C 126 (*FA:ED* 2, 330).
[73] LMj 7:9 (*FA:ED* 2, 582-83).

Cross."[74] Finally, Francis intoned the psalm *Voce mea* with his last breath: "Set free my soul from its prison so that I may celebrate your name; the just wait for me and among them you will give me my recompense." Night had fallen. It was October 3, 1226. He died while singing.

He was entombed in the church of Saint George. Two years later he was canonized. And on May 25, 1230, his relics were transferred to the basilica in Assisi where they are still venerated.

The First Generation of Franciscans

A message too new and too solid, disciples too numerous, beginnings too varied and too unshaped, not enough time to set things sufficiently in order – at Francis's death conflict could not help but erupt.

To tell the truth, even if history records struggles that were indeed lively, we should not overexaggerate their importance. While the two extremist branches of the order exchanged hard words and often venomous writings, the great majority continued to walk the path traced out by their founder. The order was certainly experiencing a painful malaise, but it was helpful because it allowed the brothers to really clarify some ideas.

This was not due to a lack of generosity or fervor, but to a narrowness of spirit and lack of openness of heart. The great fault of certain brothers was to try to justify concrete practice by an appeal to principles and to attempt to define a Franciscan in negative or reactionary terms instead of accepting everything and working with it. Yet Francis had one day indicated the method to be followed in order to preserve unity. He had described the true Friar Minor not in terms of a catalog of faults to be avoided, but as the sum of all that was positive in each of his companions: "The true Friar Minor should love poverty like Brother Bernard, and prayer like Brother Rufino who prays even while asleep; he should

---

[74] 1C 112 (*FA:ED* 1, 279-80).

be as lost in God as Brother Giles, as courteous as Brother
Angelo, and as patient as Brother Juniper; he should possess
the purity and ingenuity of Brother Leo, the distinction and
good sense of Brother Masseo, and should finally resemble
Brother Lucidus in detachment, who never stays more than
one month in the same place because we have no permanent
dwelling here below."[75] This was a sensitive and realistic way
of developing the gospel theme: "There are many dwellings
in my father's house." Unfortunately, instead of going along
in this way, every trick was tried to oppose it.

At the heart of the conflict were, on the one hand, two
texts which everyone held dear and, on the other, partisans
of two tendencies, different people arguing their positions on
the basis of these texts.

What an end for the texts that Francis begged to be accepted without interpretations! When a rule begins with the
words, "The life of the Friars Minor consists in following the
gospel," it is clear that the twelve brief chapters that follow
cannot possibly exhaust the initial application of this massive affirmation. It is as impossible to imagine that one could
finish applying or living this rule of life as it would be to
imagine one had finally applied or lived the gospel. All the
more so, since these chapters were often responses to particular situations overcome here and there, for which Rome had
ratified and universalized a solution. Yet at the end of his life,
Francis reviewed and developed the formulation of his ideal:
He did so in the *Testament,* which some wanted to use like
a cannon against the legal armada of the twelve chapters in
the Rule of 1223.

The two initial antagonists were friends of Saint Francis:
Brother Leo and Brother Elias. The saint had confided his
soul to the first by choosing him as his confessor; to the second he confided the destiny of the order, since he was named
general minister during the lifetime of the founder. Leo, mystical and scrupulous, kept the least remembrance of the past
in his heart, all the words and actions of his father, as if there
were not a kind of sterile pharisaism involved in turning in

---

[75] 2MP 85 (*FA:ED* 3, 333).

upon immutable positions while all else evolves. Elias, practical and ambitious, thought of little but the grandiose future of the order whose reins he held, and used all his political and financial relationships to this end, as if there were no risk that he could become lost by trying to adapt without being faithful to the order's roots. He gave himself over to outrages like the building of the *Sacro Convento*, which was seen as the very symbol of his apostasy.[76] It was a case of authority in disarray. Small wonder that some brothers would put their ideal of poverty above obedience, including obedience to the church, and even above charity. It was impossible to have been in more flagrant contradiction with Francis's ideals.

Those who held to the primitive tradition drew the name *Zelanti* and, later, *Observants*. They were withdrawn into hermitages most of the time and left to the *Conventuals* the urban convents and a limited right to property recognized by Rome. The crisis was complicated further when the Observants were tainted by Joachimism,[77] affirming that the age of the Holy Spirit began with Saint Francis and calling themselves *Spirituals*. Some even resisted the authority of the pope and were later caught up in the sects condemned in 1317 by the decree *Quorumdam* issued by John XXII: Fraticelli, Brothers of the Poor Life, etc.

The first Franciscan community here underwent a crisis similar to that of the first Christian community. But, no more than the episode of Ananias and Saphire proved the impossibility of practicing the gospel did the quarrel of the Spirituals detract anything at all from the Franciscan ideal.

---

[76] In his defense it must be noted that the pope himself wanted a convent spacious enough to house the pontifical court when he visited. But couldn't Elias have refused? Later, Saint Clare held out against a pope who wanted her to accept some revenues, and she obtained the "privilege of poverty."

[77] From the name of Joachim (1145-1202), a Cistercian and founder of the abbey of Fiore, in Calabria. He divided human history into three ages: the pre-Christian era (that of the Father, dominated by the laity); the Christian era (that of the Son, dominated by clerics); and the era of the Holy Spirit when a new wave of monk-prophets would cover the earth. The Spirituals imagined (and hence their name) that they were this awaited and proclaimed order.

For the latter was truly alive in 1260 with Saint Bonaventure whose genius and holiness made him the second founder of the order. He managed first of all to purge the remnants of Joachimism that threatened to drag the better elements into heresy. His goodness won him the confidence of all concerned, his common sense did the rest, and the Constitutions he published in 1260 are a masterpiece of respect for the spirit as well as the letter of the rule, in addition to being a monument of prudence and organization.

Bonaventure also had his effect upon spiritual doctrine: We would not really know the Franciscan ideal if this privileged witness had not transmitted a good deal of the tradition to us in the form of historical works like his *Life of Saint Francis,* didactic works like the *Sermon on the Rule,* or polemical works like his *Apologia of the Poor* and *Answer to Three Questions* raised by a master at the university. If we needed a practical confirmation of the value of his works, it would be found in this fact: that the many reforms that spring up throughout the history of the order, attempting to go back to the "primitive purity" of the ideal, all eventually come back to the Bonaventurian adaptation once they lose their local character and constraint, once the number of their followers increases.

Whatever dynamism and solidity the Franciscan Order still possesses today will be maintained by a firm and sure grasp of the two-polar notion: the high mysticism of its ideal and the concrete sense of the human realities in which this ideal is incarnated. The personal charism of each brother adds its originality to the sum of these elements. But, thanks to Saint Bonaventure, after 700 years a little of Francis's blood still runs in the veins of his great family.

III. THE SPIRITUAL UNIVERSE OF SAINT FRANCIS

One feels hesitant about setting a sacrilegious hand to the *Writings* of Saint Francis when analyzing them; their overall harmony and coherence is so perfect. It is something like the shudder one might feel at performing an autopsy on a living body or shredding to pieces the canvas of a great master. But without falling into a systematic reduction of the whole to a few vague and abstract propositions, we can try to rediscover in the written expression of the faith of the Poverello certain constants already picked up by his biographers. We discover therein a spiritual life of surprising unity.

The Composition of the Writings

At first glance, some superficial surprises strike the reader and raise problems concerning the mode of composition (questions which we can only touch upon here).

Except for such-and-such a letter, the written work of Saint Francis consists of *short pieces* – one might even be tempted to say, *odd* pieces. This fact is due not to a lack of inspiration on the author's part, but to the method used in compiling the collection and to the filial piety of those who wanted to lose nothing of the sermons, letters, and prayers of their father. For a son, the least fragment is a treasure. We should thus be thankful to those who salvaged these bits and pieces. Certain admonitions two or three verses long sometimes condense a spiritual doctrine that suffices to rank Saint Francis among the greatest mystics.

A closer reading reveals a certain *diversity of styles* in the *Writings:* stark or even harsh, as in the *Testament,* juridical and occasionally categorical, as in the *Rule of 1223*, clear as crystal as in the *Adoramus Te* and some of the litanical prayers, or somewhat precious and affected as in the *Absorbeat* and the paraphrase of the Our Father. These variations reflect the evolution of the spirit of the author in the course of his life, the diversity of his sources of inspiration, and also the diversity of his secretaries. For Francis, even before his total blindness, sought the help of his companions and above all his confessor Leo to whom he dictated his words, leaving some initiative to the scribe as was the custom at that time. The latter, fortunately, influenced his expression only slightly, as the autobiographical writings we have made clear. Even the rule, although put together by the pontifical Chancery, allows us to truly meet the saint himself at the turning of every page.

One discovery which should not surprise us: there are numerous quotations from the New Testament which, far from being simply illustrations of his thought,[78] are part and parcel of it. The gospel was not an arsenal of well-labeled quotations for him. He leaves this approach to certain commentators who fool around with any text, sacred or not, with little respect. The identification of the thought of the saint with that of the New Testament is not what is least appealing in the *Writings.* He would willingly subscribe to this sentence from a writer who is nevertheless considerably removed from him in time and preoccupation: "I never open the gospel without feeling directly and personally challenged; and I believe that

---

[78] Certain of these, it is true, are only ornaments in the *Early Rule,* but these are due to the influence of Caesar of Spire: cf. Jordan of Giano, *Chronicle,* 19, in *XIIIth Century Chronicles* (Chicago: Franciscan Herald Press, 1961), 36-38. Sabatier has already pointed out: "When Saint Francis reads the bible he does not try to fill up his memory, but to discover a light and a force; his action – for it is but one – aims to be *incorporated into the eternal life of the church*" (Speech given in Canterbury Cathedral). And Saint Francis of Sales: "The great Saint Francis was admirable in his assimilation of the sacred maxims he heard in the gospel; for he changed himself so much through them that he was no longer himself but became what the maxims signified…. O God, how happy he was to have digested this holy word so well that he became transformed into it!" (*Works,* vol. 4).

one hears nothing of the teaching of Christ from the moment that one detracts from or defers its urgency."[79]

The *liturgy* is also one of the more important sources of inspiration in the composition of the *Writings*. Not only did it furnish Francis with a number of his favorite biblical texts; not only did the spirit of the liturgy preside over the elaboration of the *Office of the Passion;* but it is the liturgy which also supplied him with a framework for his thought, as in the various "thanksgivings" derived in great part from the prefaces of the Mass, or as in the prayers of praise in which one can detect the imprint of the *Gloria,* the *Te Deum* or the *Canticle of David.* It was the liturgy, specifically the readings in the breviary, which suggested certain patristic themes; whence the Augustinian flavor of many passages. Finally, the liturgy has, so to speak, molded into a form uniquely its own, some prayers of Saint Francis where the lyrical quality is admirably wedded to the restraint of Gregorian prayers, the adoration of the Most High to affection for the Father.

Another general impression: the striking *simplicity of doctrine.* The words are always very concrete; the steps advanced for approaching God are devoid of detours and complications; the interpretations of the word of God downplay useless knowledge and subtlety. It was with this in mind that Saint Francis referred to himself as "idiota," and repudiated empty science. But it was to the advantage of these two great Ladies whom he welcomed with the exquisite and inseparable salutation:

"Hail Queen *Wisdom,* may the Lord save you,
with your sister, holy and pure *Simplicity!*"

The Major Themes of the Writings

Saint Francis's intuitive and acquired wisdom has its origins not in a frozen *Cogito,* but in a person, in the one who is the very wisdom of the Father. The entire spiritual universe of Saint Francis is based on a personal and living experi-

---

[79] A. Gide, *Journal* (Paris: Gallimard, 1951), 621.

ence, namely, his encounter with the person of Jesus Christ. Therein is lodged the secret of the internal logic of his spirituality.[80] One could even say that his entire life consisted in variations upon this one theme: the Christ.

Francis was a man at once simple and passionate. We can thus be sure that his spirituality would be limited, on the one hand, to what is essential and not intellectual; and, on the other hand, to the holistic and integral, to the ultimate and absolute. He leaves out nothing in the plan of God but sums it up in one vision, one object: Christ. In the history of salvation (and of his salvation) Francis does not separate creation-revelation-incarnation-redemption. God always gives himself totally and to all in Jesus Christ.

In Christ, Francis discovers both the sublimity of God (his transcendence) and what he calls the humility of God (his immanence). For him these are two inseparable dimensions of the mystery of the word become incarnate through love. For him, God's greatness can never be discovered so well as by the way in which he became our servant. For him, the clearest light shed on God's greatness radiates from the self emptying of Christ in the manger and on the cross. As the visible expression of God, this is the means by which he comes down to the level of sinful humanity. Francis can take in these polar extremes in one glance because he understands that the bond between them is the person of Jesus Christ; that which fills the in-between is love.

And Francis, who is aware of having received everything that he has, finds all of his happiness in acknowledging, proclaiming, sharing, and rendering back what he has received. He, too, finds his joy in love; to the extent of giving away everything, of becoming forever indebted to love.

---

[80] What we understand by spirituality in its broader sense is a particular way of approaching God. It is at once a deep experience and a particular style of life, a philosophy and an art, an undertaking that includes prayer as well as lifestyle, contemplation as well as asceticism. It is the original creation of a whole personal religious universe. One can thus readily see how the themes presented successively in the following pages constitute artificial divisions; even so, they provide an opportunity for us to get a clearer idea of the special coloration of the saint's spirituality.

This basic discovery reverberates through every part of his meditation and behavior. Let us review them quickly, invited to do so by the Poverello who knew how to discover the multiple dimensions of the Godman and who in his prayer loved to move from one to the other. "There he would give answer to his judge, there he would offer petitions to his father; there he would speak intimately with his friend; there he would rejoice with the bridegroom."[81]

1. The Incarnation

For Francis, Christ is primarily *the man Jesus,*[82] the son of the Virgin Mary. His religion is a historical one with a central event: the incarnation of the Son of God. Instinctively he goes to the fundamental belief that resolves every question and stimulates every action: Christ become man.

Francis has a visual temperament. He needs to use his imagination. Thus, he strongly emphasizes the events of the earthly life of Christ. Whence, in his *Writings,* the large number of phrases like "Let us consider, my brothers"[83] and "Let us remember, my brothers"[84] which introduce a development of one dimension of the human life of Christ. Whence, also, his need to express himself through actions, gestures, etc., to reenact one scene or another; for example, the nativity at Greccio.[85]

---

[81] 2C 95 (*FA:ED* 2, 309-10).

[82] 1 Timothy 2,5. The historical importance of this attitude should be of no less note to us than its spiritual importance. In the face of docetic Catharism, the church's insistence on the humanity of Christ comes to light. F. Heer points out this significant fact concerning Germany in particular: "From the days of Notker until the beginning of the twelfth century one could never find the name of Jesus – the name Christ bore as man – in the literature," in *Aufgang Europas* (Vienna-Zurich: Europa Verlag, 1949), 110. Fortunately, in France there was Saint Bernard: "*Si scribas, non sapit mihi nisi legero ibi Jesum,*" in *Sermo* 15 *super Canticum.*

[83] Adm 6 (*FA:ED* 1, 131); ER 22 (*FA:ED* 1, 79), etc.

[84] ER 9 (*FA:ED* 1, 70), etc.

[85] L. Gillet, *Sur les pas de saint François* (Paris: Plon, 1926), 131-33: "Francis possessed this instinct for pantomime to a remarkable degree: the Italian sense of movement that transforms the briefest narrative into a spectacle. A surprising sense for the theatrical enlivened this small, sickly, extraordinary man. There was a kind of genius that drove him at all times,

Among all the events of the life of Christ, the one he remembered most was the birth at Bethlehem: "The birthday of the child Jesus Francis observed with inexpressible eagerness over all other feasts saying that it was the feast of feasts, on which God, having become a tiny infant, clung to human breasts."[86]

Naive devotion? Not at all. It is the undertaking of a faith that is simple, to be sure, but also true and absolute: "Totally respecting the way in which God gives himself to us, Francis's devotion reaches out to meet the Incarnation. Since the love of God wanted to become perceptible, visible, and tangible, is there any better attitude for man than to perceive and touch?"[87] Francis would have been astonished if he had been told that his faith, that of a simple man, was thus like that of Saint John: "What we have heard, what we have seen with our eyes, what our hands have touched of the Word of Life ... by this we have known the love of God."[88]

But the incarnation is not limited to Christmas. The human condition accepted by Christ includes death. It is thus, in all its far-reaching implications and its later development, that Francis envisaged the incarnation as leading up to and including the cross. He meditated on its mystery so deeply that at the end of his life he could respond to a brother who offered a commentary on holy scripture to him: "It is good to read the testimonies of the scriptures; it is good to seek the Lord our God in them. As for me, however, I have already made so much of scripture my own that I have more than enough to meditate on and revolve in my mind. I need no more, son; I know Christ, the poor crucified one."[89]

---

out of his need for self-expression, to concoct situations: daring, striking, singular, and terrible scenes that shook up his audience, leaving it wonder struck. He had the gift of being able to instantly organize an idea, dramatize it, and make it a one-act presentation both striking and moving."

[86] 2C 99 (*FA:ED* 2, 312-13). Saint Francis's great Marian devotion was rooted in these depths. In Mary, he venerated the one by whom the Lord of majesty became our brother.

[87] I.-E. Motte, "Epiphanie du Seigneur," in *Cahiers de vie franciscaine* 32 (1961): 194.

[88] 1 John 1:1 and 3:16.

[89] 2C 105 (*FA:ED* 2, 316).

Theologians, popular preachers, and above all the *Meditations of the Life of Christ*,[90] the whole Franciscan school, following its founder, does nothing but develop this theme of the incarnation, apart from occasionally stressing the redemptive death. For three centuries medieval piety and European art received a new impetus from it. What has sometimes been disparagingly labeled "Franciscan romanticism" was in reality but a return to and emphasis upon the very heart of our faith: the Incarnation of the Son of God.

2. Glory

Francis's Christ is not only the man Jesus Christ, but also and inseparably the *Lord of Glory*. He is the one whom "you should fall to the ground and adore with fear and reverence at the sound of his name; the Lord Jesus Christ, Son of the Most High, is his name ..."[91]

Molded by the liturgy where the word "glory" punctuates or ends so many prayers, Francis likewise adopts the doxology as his favorite prayer. To the *Gloria* of the psalms, he adds his own: "Let us bless the Father," and "Blessed are you, my Lord."

The liturgy also teaches him to read the Bible from this point of view. In his *Writings* he often borrows texts from the Apocalypse, such as the poem to the glory of Christ quoted in the Missal or in the breviary. The liturgy "opened up the scriptures" for him and he discovered in them the God to whom alone belongs glory. From it he drew his sense of adoration. The expression "kingdom of God" had as its background for him all the manifestations of glory in the Old and New Testaments: from Sinai to the Last judgment, by way of Mount Tabor.

The liturgy, finally, taught him how to read the world. He was naturally inclined to this; the age in which he lived was

---

[90] Long attributed to Saint Bonaventure, their true author is the Franciscan John de Caulibus: *Meditations on the Life of Christ*, translated by A. Miller and F.X. Taney (Glendale Heights, Illinois: Pegasus Press, 2000). They had considerable influence on medieval art.

[91] LtOrd 4 (*FA:ED* 2, 116).

likewise enamored with symbolism. This attitude was also strengthened in him each time he sang: "The heavens speak of the glory of God"[92] and "The universe is filled with your glory";[93] or when he read: "If such are the fringes of the cloak of my Father, what then must be the splendor of his face."[94]

Even in his *Office of the Passion* Francis cannot bring himself to disassociate death from glory. The psalm written for None – the hour when Jesus gave over his spirit – ends with five verses dedicated to the expectation of the resurrection and the parousia. And the psalm for Vespers is a joyous outburst centering on the triumph of Christ, the *regnavit a ligno* ("It is by the cross that he has become our king.") A basic reference for a true understanding of Francis's religious mentality, this office never considers the "sorrowful passion" without immediately and clearly evoking "the most blessed passion." A deep feeling of sympathy for the man of sorrows is always accompanied by the boundless joy aroused by the victory of the redeemer. This theme of glory and of final Passover serves as a background for Francis's magnificent celebration of his own death. He acted out his final "mystery" while reenacting at the same time the mysteries of the death and resurrection of Christ.

It must be emphasized that Francis's meditation expands the mystery of redemption to include the return of Christ at the end of time and the fulfillment of the world in glory. This dimension is always in his mind when he speaks of Christ the "savior." Such is the meaning of his invocation at the beginning of the *Prayer Inspired by the Our Father*, which enumerates the threefold action of God as creator, redeemer, and savior. So, too, with the psalm he wrote for the feast of the Ascension which ends with a note of hope and jubilant certainty: "And we know that he comes." Thomas of Celano, a witness to this enthusiasm, describes it in all its richness: "When he pronounced your name, Lord, he seemed like a man of the world to come."[95]

---

[92] Psalm 19:2.
[93] Isaiah 6:3.
[94] Job 26:14.
[95] 1C 82 (*FA:ED* 1, 251).

Once again, Saint Francis when dealing with the theme of the incarnation joins with the thought of Saint John who assembles in one verse the two basic dimensions of revelation: "The word was made *flesh* ... and we have seen his *glory*."[96]

This is the supernatural basis of Saint Francis's deep optimism: an optimism based not on strong physical health but on a faith firmly anchored in the victory of Christ. Such is also the secret as he confided one day to Brother Leo of his prayer of adoration and praise.[97] Through the flesh and through the glory of Christ, he finally knew who he was and who God is!

3. Gift

Francis's Christ is also the *mediator*, the one through whom all benefits come to us: both the gifts of God and their being given back to God, their restoration by men and women. For if Christ, as we have seen, is the point of intersection where the two "dimensions" of God (transcendence and immanence, greatness and humility) intersect in love, he is also the place of encounter between God and man, between God and all of creation.

Francis called God "our great almsgiver."[98] With this phrase he expressed his total vision of the world. Indeed, convinced that he had received everything gratuitously, as a totally undeserved alms, he could not remain indifferent to anything, either people or things. He walked through a kind of enchanted forest where every object was a sign of God's kindness. What a gift it is when everything is a symbol and an expression of love, where even sin and suffering wind up speaking of redemption! For him nature had truly become a temple once again. He looked at it with the very eyes of God and like God he saw that it was good. He was like a child full of wonder, breathless and in ecstasy before the toys which he had received and which were so many proofs of the love of his parents. He lived the mysteries of creation and redemp-

---

[96] John 1:14.
[97] DBF 9 (*FA:ED* 3, 452-58).
[98] 2C 77 (*FA:ED* 2, 298).

tion with great intensity; he enumerated all their benefits: life, understanding, animals and all things, all the graces of salvation, revelation, the cross, and the sacraments ...

He does not limit himself to contemplation. This vision determines concrete attitudes for him, a veneration for every creature, even the most humble, since it was a creation of God. He respected even the smallest bit of parchment since it bore a word given by God.

He lived in an attitude of deep poverty, a poverty which was not a stripping-away but a restoration to God of what he has given. One of his favorite expressions was "to render all good back to the Lord" and he applied it to intellectual and spiritual values as well as material ones. He considered vanity and envy robbery because through them we seek to appropriate for ourselves the good that the Lord has placed in us and others. Humility is not a debasing of ourselves but a simple acknowledgment that we possess nothing of our own except our sins and vices.

Everything is a gift through Jesus Christ: everything must be given back through Jesus Christ. In the midst of this coming and going how could Francis not be happy in spite of sufferings, sicknesses, and imperfections, for these also converge for one's good? He multiplied the joys of giving and receiving, the joys of feeling loved because one has received so much, with the joy of loving to the extent of giving up everything.

4. The Word of God

In addition to the "mediator of being," Francis's Christ is also the "mediator of understanding," since he is the Word of God himself.[99] Receptivity to revelation is another primordial dimension of the religion and spirituality of Francis.

Up to the moment of the dialogue at San Damiano, he had seen many crucifixes; but then he heard the voice of the crucified one, and every subsequent word of Christ reverberated in his soul like an echo of the first calling. His attention

---

[99] 2LtF 3 (*FA:ED* 2, 45).

to the word of God is not, even so, based on this private revelation but rather upon the universal revelation that was the object of his heartfelt search, and especially upon the gospel, the word of God to the world. "He was not a deaf hearer of the gospel."[100]

When he seeks to define life in fraternities, a few words suffice: to observe the holy gospel. When he wants to justify a commandment or a counsel he finds nothing stronger or more binding than: "For the Lord has said ..."[101] He has such trust in the value of the word of God that in order to discover with Brother Bernard what was to be his spiritual direction, he used an almost superstitious practice: opening the book of the gospel, at random, three times.[102]

This veneration for the word of God was also a respect for the writings wherever they appeared, for the theologians who are its ministers, and for the church that nourishes us like a mother with her milk. This was a leitmotif for Francis. He was even scrupulous, or nearly so, in his veneration, and this was a courageous attitude for a time when lack of constraint in these areas was indeed quite shocking.[103]

---

[100] 1C 22 (*FA:ED* 1, 202).

[101] ER 16 and 17 (*FA:ED* 1, 74-77), LR 10 (*FA:ED* 1, 105), etc.

[102] 2C 15 (*FA:ED* 2, 253-54). This practice of drawing by lots, then very popular, was condemned by the church; but only, it seems, when it was a question of discovering in the gospel something the latter was never intended to reveal (e.g., the correct choice in an election, a justification for a specification, a prediction about one's death, a political decision, or even the selection of some merchandise).

[103] The *Letter to the Clergy*, in particular, clearly confirms what the tales tell us. In those days an inquisitor rose up against the abuses of "those who do not renew consecrated hosts in time, so that they swarm with worms; who frequently let the body and blood of the Lord fall to the ground; who preserve the Most Blessed Sacrament in their room or in a tree of the garden; who, while visiting the sick, hang the Holy Eucharist up in a room and go to the tavern; who administer the Sacrament to public sinners and refuse it to the worthy; who celebrate Mass while living in notorious sin; who use adulterated wine for the Sacrifice, pour more water than wine into the chalice, and celebrate again after consuming the ablution; who read several Masses on one day without reason; who protract the Mass unduly by excessively long and confused singing; who establish taverns in the churches and render unseemly plays therein." Cf. H. Felder, *The Ideals of Saint Francis of Assisi* (Chicago: Franciscan Herald Press, 1982), 447.

"He who is from God listens to the word of God," he re-
peats with Saint John.[104] Because for him the word of God
was not only a vector of understanding but above all a source
of the faith that saves. "No one can be saved except by the
blood of our Lord Jesus Christ and by his holy words."[105] And
while this "word that saves" is received as a gift from God
along with the other wonders of Christian life, he knows that
he cannot possess it. The way to "render it back to God," as
with all other benefits, is to communicate it to our brothers
and sisters. It is with this in mind that he quotes the priestly
prayer of Jesus applying it to himself: "The words which you
have given to me, I have given to them. They have received it
and have believed; sanctify them."

5. Eucharist

Francis's Christ is the Christ who gives himself not only
in his words but also in the sacraments, in particular in that
of the Eucharist.

Often, when he relates a deed or a decision of Christ especially in connection with the sacraments Francis comple-
ments the verb he uses with *pro nobis,* "for us." His frequent
use of this expression manifests a desire to contemplate at
once both the deed and the deep motivation behind it: love
for men and women. This thought filled him with deep wonder and thanksgiving. In the same way, Francis meditated
upon the verse, "The Lord God offers himself to us as to his
children,"[106] in its relation to the Eucharist.

Let us not forget that Francis was a deacon and could
therefore "touch the Lord with his hands."[107] Let us not forget
that he had a special love for France as the country which
had the strongest veneration for the Holy Eucharist,[108] aware
as he was of the neglect around him which often bordered on
profanation, "because in this world I cannot see the most high

---

[104] John 8:47; LtOrd 34 (*FA:ED* 1, 119).
[105] 2LtF 34 (*FA:ED* 1, 47).
[106] Hebrew 12:7; LtOrd 11 (*FA:ED* 1, 117).
[107] 1LtCl 8 (*FA:ED* 1, 53); 2LtCl 8 (*FA:ED* 1, 54).
[108] AC 108 (*FA:ED* 2, 214).

son of God with my own eyes, except for his most holy body and blood."[109] Then what respect it should be shown! When he visited the churches of Umbria he often took a broom with him and considered it his duty to do what he could to clean them.

Yet these are only external manifestations of respect. One must first of all celebrate the sacrifice[110] and receive communion worthily:[111] in a state of grace, to be sure, but in a state of faith as well, believing that this is truly the body of the son of God. One of Francis's expressions in this respect is very daring but astonishingly logical. To receive communion one must have the Holy Spirit with oneself for he is the one who receives the body of the Lord. At a time so torn by quarrels on this subject, such a faith in the real presence was truly meritorious.

Purity and faith but thanksgiving, too. What beautiful antiphons, worthy of the Office of Christ the King, could be gleaned from his letters! Caught up in his inspiration, he sometimes forgets whom he is addressing and lets himself be swept away by the subject:

The world should tremble and heaven rejoice when Christ the son of the living God is present on the altar in the hand of the priest. What wonderful majesty! What stupendous condescension. O sublime humility! O humble sublimity! That the Lord of the whole universe, the son of God, should humble himself like this and hide under the form of a little bread, for our salvation. Look at God's condescension my brothers, and pour out your hearts before him. Humble yourselves so that you may be exalted by him. Keep nothing for yourselves so that the one who has given himself wholly to you may receive you wholly.[112]

---

[109] Test 10 (*FA:ED* 1, 125).
[110] LtOrd 14 (*FA:ED* 1, 117).
[111] 2LtF 24 (*FA:ED* 1, 47).
[112] LtOrd 26-29 (*FA:ED* 1, 118).

We can imagine something of what his thanksgiving must have been like by reading his brief commentary on the fifth petition of the Our Father:

> Give us this day our daily bread,
> your own beloved Son, our Lord Jesus Christ,
> so that we might always remember, understand, and
> appreciate the love he showed for us,
> and all that he did, said, or suffered for us.[113]

6. Pilgrimage

The Christ of Francis is truth (word) and life (Eucharist); he is also the way.

"No one comes to the Father but through me!" This sentence from Saint John which begins the collection of his *Writings*[114] had resonances which are difficult for us to imagine, as well as very concrete extensions of meaning for the saint. Not only did he reject any other mediator as a way to God; not only did he acknowledge no other itinerary for his soul than the gospel; but his status as an exile gave him the obligation to truly *journey* toward the Father.

This was already for him a way of imitating Christ:

> When speaking about poverty to the brothers, Francis often quoted the words of the gospel, 'Foxes have holes, and the birds of the air their nests; the Son of Man has nowhere to lay his head'[115] and he gave orders that the houses they built should be small, like those of the poor. There the brothers should live not as if the house belonged to them, but as strangers and pilgrims in a house which was not their own. It was part of a pilgrim's life, he said, to shelter under another's roof and pass on peacefully, longing for home.[116]

---

[113] PrOF 6 (*FA:ED* 1, 159).
[114] Adm I (*FA:ED* 1, 128).
[115] Matthew 8:20.
[116] LMj 7:2 (*FA:ED* 2, 578).

This was also with a paschal resonance a way of gaining heaven, our Promised Land. "He spoke to them, telling them how they should pass through this world like strangers and pilgrims and celebrate the Lord's Pasch continually in poverty of spirit, like the Hebrews[117] in the desert, the Pasch that is his passage from this world to the Father."[118] He went so far as to include *sollicitudo,* the desire for elsewhere, as one of the qualities of a true Friar Minor; a restlessness which led some to become gyrovagues.[119]

A very revealing detail: "This man not only despised arrogance with regard to houses, but he also had a great horror of many and exquisite furnishings in the houses. He wanted nothing on the table, nothing in the utensils, that would bring back memories of the world. Everything should show forth our state as pilgrims, everything bespeak our exile."[120] The eschatological meaning of poverty is thus strongly emphasized: "It is poverty which leads us to the land of the living!"[121]

This pilgrimage is eschatological due to its goal, ascetical due to the penance and poverty which are its necessary accompaniment, and apostolic in its obedience to Christ's command: "Go and teach all nations!" In obedience to the command of Innocent III as well: "Go, with the Lord as your companion!"[122] In one of the first revelations that he received concerning the future of his itinerant fraternity, had not Francis seen his brothers coming and going everywhere: "And behold the sound of them is in my ears!"[123]

But if the pilgrimage requires a stripping-away of all that burdens the journey ("It is naked that one must go to the Lord"[124]), it brings with it the joy of delighting in all of cre-

---

[117] Hebrew, in the sense of a traveler, passenger, or pilgrim, according to the *Etymologies* of Saint Jerome and Saint Isidore of Seville. Cf. E. Gilson, "Quelques Raisonnements scripturaires au moyen âge," in *Les Idées et les Lettres* (Paris: J. Vrin, 1932), 165 ff.

[118] LMj 7:9 (*FA:ED* 2, 582-83).

[119] 2MP 85 (*FA:ED* 3, 333).

[120] 2C 60 (*FA:ED* 2, 287).

[121] LR 6:5 (*FA:ED* 1, 103).

[122] 1C 33 (*FA:ED* 1, 212).

[123] 1C 27 (*FA:ED* 1, 206).

[124] 2C 12 (*FA:ED* 2, 251).

ation not as a settled owner but as a poor man filled with
gifts like the Hebrews in the desert feasting on manna:

> Hurrying to leave this world inasmuch as it is the
> place of exile of our pilgrimage, this blessed traveler
> was yet helped not a little by the things that are in
> the world ... he used it as a very bright image of the
> goodness of God.... He rejoiced in all the works of the
> hands of the Lord.... Through his footprints impressed
> upon things he followed the beloved everywhere.[125]

One is not a true pilgrim until one has felt the need to sing.

Let us point out, finally, that a pilgrimage presupposes
a concrete goal, a privileged place, a theatre of more abun-
dant graces from the Lord or a more striking symbol of the
heavenly Jerusalem toward which we aspire. Francis visited
Rome, Saint James of Compostella, and Jerusalem, those
great centers of Christendom. A quest for Christ on the high-
ways and in the sanctuaries: a translation of this other, more
interior quest which drove him to "follow in the footsteps of
the Lord."

7. Imitation

The Christ of Francis is *drawing and transforming love.*
He who loves Christ desires to resemble him and allow himself to be shaped by him.

Saint Clare, faithful echo of the teachings of the Poverello, provides us with the most beautiful expression of this
teaching on imitation. She writes to Agnes of Prague: "Place
your spirit before Christ who is the mirror of the Eternal
One, let your soul bask in the splendor of his glory, unite your
heart with he who is the image of the divine essence, and
thanks to this contemplation you will be wholly transformed
into the resemblance of his divinity."[126]

---

[125] 2C 165 (*FA:ED* 2, 353).

[126] Clare of Assisi, Third Letter to Agnes of Prague 12-13, in *Clare of
Assisi: Early Documents*, ed. R. J. Armstrong (New York: New City Press,
2006), 51.

The imitation of Christ: this expression is not found as such in the *Writings*. Francis prefers to use either a quote from scripture – "to walk in his footsteps"[127] or "to come after him"[128] – or an expression with a definite complement – to follow the teachings and the example of our Lord Jesus Christ, to follow the poverty of Jesus Christ.... He often insists on the exemplary value for us of all the deeds of the life of Christ.

Even to the last detail, he tried to make his life conform to him: "Once when he was sitting at dinner, a certain brother talked about the poverty of the Blessed Virgin[129] and recalled the want of Christ, her Son. Francis immediately arose from the table and, with great sighs and many tears, ate the rest of his bread on the bare ground."[130]

But the imitation of the deeds of the Lord is of no value without interior conformity.[131] Francis, for example, is obedient because Christ placed his will in that of the Father, saying: "Father, may your will be done!"[132] and, doing this, he knows that he becomes the brother of Christ.[133] Nor, for Francis, is poverty considered as a means. It, too, is only a consequence flowing from his love for the poor Christ. It is not ascetical ("the less I possess, the more I am in possession of myself"!): This would be pure stoicism; it is not primarily apostolic ("the more I am detached, the more I am free for the souls of others"!); by its nature it is essentially mystical. Francis contemplates the Christ whom he loves and this suffices to dictate his behavior: imitation.

---

[127] 1 Peter 2:21.

[128] Matt 19:21; 16:24; Luke 14:26. All cited in the *Early Rule*. In the *Writings,* despite their brevity, *sequi* (to follow) appears thirteen times, and *venire* (to come) thirty-four times.

[129] Literally: "the dear, poor, little Virgin." For the Poverello, Our Lady was the *Poverella* whose virtues he wanted to imitate.

[130] 2C 200 (*FA:ED* 2, 375).

[131] Conformity: the word and the theory were to later become very popular thanks to Barthelemeus of Pisa who wrote his *De Conformitate Vitae b. Francisci ad vitam Domini Jesu* at the end of the fourteenth century. This work was strongly criticized by the Reformation writers, in particular by E. Alber in *L'Alcoran des Cordeliers* (1733).

[132] 2LtF 10 (*FA:ED* 1, 46).

[133] 2LtF 52 (*FA:ED* 1, 49); cf. Matt 12:50.

8. Mission

For Francis, Christ is *the One sent by God*: "He left the Father's bosom to address to men the word that saves."[134] Francis would likewise become an apostle, a herald of the Great King. When one loves another, one wants him to be loved by others. This is why Francis's missionary preaching becomes a praise of Jesus Christ. When one loves his brothers, one wants them to be saved. This is why he undertakes the Tau crusade in order to put the sign of redemption on all men and women, even those most distant.

He himself wandered the roads of Italy proclaiming that Love is not loved. He went as far as Egypt to preach the faith to the Sultan. When his strength left him and he was no longer able to walk around or speak in public he still would not admit defeat but used tracts, the only means of communication left to him, to address in writing "all Christians, religious, cleric, or lay, man or woman, everyone in the whole world" in order to remain, in spite of everything, "the minister of the most sweet words of the Lord." And as a finale he blesses all those who copy this encyclical letter and send it to others.

He desired a similar orientation for his order. Each of the two rules contains a special chapter that concerns "those who go to the Saracens and other infidels." This is the first time in history that a rule for religious includes a special chapter on mission in pagan countries. His personal experience in Egypt where he was like a sheep among wolves gave him an opportunity to perfect an original evangelical missionary method, a very revolutionary one during this age of crusades; a method combining simple presence and direct action: "The brothers who go can conduct themselves among [the infidels] spiritually in two ways. One way is to avoid quarrels or disputes and be subject to every human creature for God's sake (1 Peter 2:13), so bearing witness to the fact that they are Christians. Another way is to proclaim the word of God openly, when they see that is God's will, calling on their hearers

---

[134] LMj 12:1 (*FA:ED* 2, 622).

to believe in God almighty, Father, Son, and Holy Spirit, the creator of all, and in the Son, the redeemer and savior, that they may be baptized and become Christians."[135]

The desire to give Christ is inseparable from the desire to give oneself to Christ through martyrdom if necessary. The missionaries are "not to forget that they have given themselves up completely and have handed over their whole selves to our Lord Jesus Christ." In fact, one is not "truly a friend of Christ unless one loves others as he loved them," that is to say, without limit.[136]

Francis would cry out: "I want to send all of you to heaven."[137] The first brothers possessed this same basic attitude as Thomas of Celano describes it: "They wanted to be many in oneness in order to find salvation together."[138] One sees, then, that what motivates the Franciscan missionary spirit is not an awareness of the statistics of the external needs of the church but rather of a binding, imperative, and inner need. The apostolate, like contemplation, is but an expression of the love of Christ; with the threefold motivation of making him known, of imitating him, and, if one has the chance, of rejoining him in glory by participating in his Passion.

9. The Spirit

Christ for Francis is finally *the One who gives us,* from his fullness, *the Spirit of God*, the Spirit who is freedom and liberation.

What is so appealing in the life of Saint Francis is the lightness, the spontaneity, the ease, and the naturalness we encounter on each page. But we must not allow ourselves to be misled. This does not come from the impulsive nature of one who does as he pleases according to the whim and fancy of the moment, above and beyond every law. This is not at

---

[135] ER 16:5-7 (*FA:ED* 1, 74).

[136] 2C 172 (*FA:ED* 2, 358).

[137] F. Bartholi *Tractatus de indulgentia S. Mariae de Portiuncula,* ed. P. Sabatier (Paris: Fischbacher, 1900), LIX.

[138] 1C 27 (*FA:ED* 1, 206).

all the case. It is rather the fruit of a spiritual liberation of
"the flesh" and is the result of the activity of the Spirit which
Francis allowed to live and act within him. It can never be
sufficiently emphasized that it is in relationship to obedience
that he quotes the Letter to the Galatians (5:13) where this
question is at once one of freedom, love, and spirit.[139]

The Spirit of the Lord struggles against what Francis
strangely enough calls "the spirit of the flesh."[140] In stripping
human of everything carnal, he progressively leads him to
pure simplicity and true peace of heart, frees him from slav-
ery and makes him free for God. Thus, when Francis declares,
"It is the Holy Spirit who is minister general of the order,"[141]
he does not open the way to anarchy but rather establishes
within the order a deep spiritual exigency more constraining
than any structure.

Free for God thanks to the Spirit of God. Such is the root
of Franciscan optimism. An unshakable optimism since it is
based on the very plan of God and leads us to the very heart
of the mysticism and theology of the Franciscan tradition.
The fifth Admonition is remarkable in this respect: "Try to
realize the dignity God has conferred on you. He created and
formed your body in the image of his beloved Son, and your
soul in his own likeness."[142] To be sure, sin, from our human
point of view, seems to have disturbed the plan of God by giving precedence to the flesh over the spirit; but when through
Christ the latter finds its rightful place, the human being re-
discovers the true freedom of sons, a foretaste of that which
will be his in eternal glory. This understanding covers all the
themes familiar to Francis since it places Christ at the cen-
ter as well as at the two poles of history, and since it also
considers him as filling the entire universe.

There is no other source for the free and easy way with
which Francis strolls through creation, the luminous and
fraternal regard he casts on all things. We can understand
why he ends with a triumphal Alleluia, the wonderful prayer

---

[139] ER 5:16 (*FA:ED* 1, 68).
[140] ER 17 (*FA:ED* 1, 75-76).
[141] 2C 193 (*FA:ED* 2, 371).
[142] Adm 5:1 (*FA:ED* 1, 131).

with which he thanks God for creation, for the incarnation, and for the glorious return of Christ who will come for the definitive establishment of the kingdom prepared for us since the foundation of the world.[143]

LIVING THE GOSPEL IN FRATERNITY

If we want to obtain from Francis himself a condensed formula of his ideal, we must go to the *Testament* to find it: "After the Lord had given me some brothers, the Most High revealed to me that I should live according to the holy gospel."[144] Some brothers and the gospel: two basic and inseparable elements of the life of the communities established by Francis.

Fraternity: a mystery for contemplation. Being brothers: if such is the proposed ideal, it is because it is the primary spiritual reality to be considered. For Francis, in fact, our first brother is our "brother Jesus,"[145] and the sole reason we are brothers of one another is based in the fact that Jesus is the brother of each of us. Francis never seems to tire of contemplating with rhapsodic admiration the mystery of fraternity as a gift from God: "How holy and beloved, how pleasing and restful, how peaceful, delightful, lovable and desirable above all things it is to have a brother like this, who laid down his life for us and prayed to his Father for us ..." But for him this contemplation is not limited merely to an arousing lyricism. Rather, it anchors a conviction that in turn unleashes and stimulates action. Francis knows how to make something "carnal" with the spiritual.

Fraternity: the assumption of human capacities. How could Francis have scorned feelings, for they too are a gift of the same Father. Thomas of Celano tells us as much: "Since the natural feelings of his heart already made him a brother to all creatures, it is not surprising that the charity of Christ made him more than a brother to those who are stamped

---

[143] ER 23 (*FA:ED* 1, 81-86).
[144] Test 14 (*FA:ED* 1, 125).
[145] 2LtF 56-60 (*FA:ED* 1, 49).

with the image of their creator." [146] Sensitivity, thoughtful-
ness, and cordiality are what renders his companionship, his
letters, and his words so attractive. Even when reminding
the brothers of their ideal he uses the strongest and at the
same time the most delicate comparisons: "I want that my
brothers show themselves to be children of the same mother."
[147] "They should show that they are members of the same
family."[148] "For if a mother loves and cares for her child in the
flesh, a brother should certainly love and care for his spiritual brother all the more tenderly."[149]

Fraternity: dialectic of the already and the not-yet. Faith
does not exclude a realistic outlook. If fraternity is a given,
it is also a reality that must be built up. While each brother
is already like a gift from God and a sacrament of Christ for
his brother, each brother must also *become* every day even
more a sacrament of Christ for his brother. The burden of sin
leads to division. Like a seed planted beforehand by God, the
unity of fraternity blossoms only after a great struggle. The
Rule and the Admonitions describe how fraternal love is like
a bridge between the "already you are one" and the "henceforth become one as my Father and I are one."

Fraternity: sharing and happiness. Sharing concerns daily life and events ("rejoicing at the good fortune of others, just
as if it were our own, helping them to bear their burdens"),[150]
as well as the supernatural destiny of the larger community:
"He believed that he would be without future glory unless he
made those entrusted to him glorious with him, those whom
his spirit brought forth with greater labor than a mother's
labor in giving birth to her children."[151] But this struggle is
no less a beatitude. The daily struggle to grow in fraternity
is one of the sources and one of the secrets of Franciscan
joy. "For whenever they came together anywhere, or met one
another along the way, what an explosion of love! They em-

---

[146] 2C 172 (*FA:ED* 2, 358).
[147] 2C 180 (*FA:ED* 2, 362).
[148] LR 6:7 (*FA:ED* 1, 103).
[149] LR 6:8 (*FA:ED* 1, 103).
[150] PrOF 7 (*FA:ED* 1, 159).
[151] 2C 174 (*FA:ED* 2, 359).

braced one another, shared or laughed together; they were full of life, thoughtful and kind with singleness of purpose, tireless to render service to one another. They poured out their whole affection on all the brothers."[152] These lines were written in 1228 by Thomas of Celano who was a witness to as well as an agent of the Franciscan springtime.

Fraternity: imitation and anticipation. The imitation of Christ is not limited to individual behavior. Franciscan life is a life in fraternity because Christ and his apostles lived together as brothers. Herein is a reference to the past, the *Vita Apostolica.* But herein is also a reference to the future. Fraternity is an anticipation of eternal life where we will all become brothers and sisters in a definitive way with Christ. This is the eschatological aspect of fraternity. Fraternities must be working models of the anticipated paradise.

One sentence of Saint Francis already quoted several times easily sums up the interior motive, the goal, and the final realization of life in fraternity: "Keep nothing for yourselves, so that he who has given himself wholly to you may receive you wholly."[153]

Lyricism and Spirituality

A profound lyricism, that of fulfilled lovers, undergirds the *Writings* of Saint Francis. A lyricism that can be translated by all sorts of formulas and that can disconcert only dried-up hearts and apathetic spirits. Francis enumerates at length the beauties of what he has received; he calls 'brother' everything that owes its life to the common Father; his prayer easily takes on a somewhat passionate litanical form and the repetitions seem to flow with the breathing of his soul; his exclamations are finally but a single note of adoration; and pure praise takes over when thoughts fail.

As Bremond observes so well for the French school of spirituality, his "'O's ... do not teach us Lyricism – there is no method or need for that – but they may teach us or recall

[152] 1C 38-39 (*FA:ED* 1, 217-18).
[153] LtOrd 29 (*FA:ED* 1, 118).

to us that the Christian should be lyrical in his prayer and his relations with God. The lesson is always needed. Many indeed see only an optional adornment, an unnecessary supplement, in the canticle of admiration and praise, which is nevertheless the essential of religion."[154]

The spirituality of Francis is the spirituality of a "king's son." He knows that nothing belongs to him; yet, thanks to the Father's love all graces are available. He knows this and proclaims it. It has often been repeated that once Francis understood something he immediately put it into deed. This does not go far enough. He understood the mysteries of God in his acting and became impregnated with them through his singing.

The first companions tell us how Saint Francis composed a "lauda" or canticle of praise, and taught it to his brothers. And often in the quiet of the night at the hermitage of Greccio, perched there on the hillside, the brothers sang. Then, down below, all the townsfolk, great or small, came out of their houses and lined up on the terraces to respond to the brothers, taking up the chorus which re-echoed throughout the valley: *Benedetto sia Signore Domeneddio!*[155]

Isn't there a symbol hidden here? Every deed of Francis and his brothers seems to have been nothing but a song: one so vigorous, so beautiful, and so convincing that it awakens in all men and women the sense of God and teaches them its praises, rendering all good back to God. "To the praise of Christ": This is the formula that closes each of the chapters of the *Fioretti*, the Little Flowers; such, indeed, was the mission of Francis; and such, thanks to his *Writings,* testimony to his faith and his love, is the mission he perpetuates among us.

---

[154] H. Bremond, *A Literary History of Religious Thought in France from the Wars of Religion down to Our Own Times,* Vol. III (New York: The McMillan Co., 1928), 106-07.

[155] AC 74 (*FA:ED* 2, 177).

SUGGESTED READINGS

1. Early Documents

All the early documents, including the writings of Francis himself, the remembrances of his companions, and the works of his first biographers, can be found in the following work:

Francis of Assisi: Early Documents, edited by R. J. Armstrong, J. A. W. Hellmann, W. J. Short, 3 volumes (New York: New City Press, 1999-2001)

2. Modern Biographies

P. Sabatier, *Life of St Francis of Assisi* (Charleston: Nabu Press, 2011).

J. Jørgensen, *Francis of Assisi: A Biography* (Charleston: Nabu Press, 2011).

O. Englebert, *Saint Francis of Assisi: A Biography* (Cincinnati: St. Anthony Messenger Press, 1979).

R. Manselli, *St. Francis of Assisi* (Chicago: Franciscan Herald Press, 1984; St. Bonaventure, NY: Franciscan Institute Publications, 2007).

A. House, *Francis of Assisi: A Revolutionary Life* (Mahwah: Paulist Press, 2003).

D. Spoto, *Reluctant Saint: The Life of Francis of Assisi* (New York: Penguin, 2003).

A. Vauchez, *Francis of Assisi: The Life and Afterlife of a Medieval Saint* (New Haven: Yale University Press, 2012).

A. Thompson, *Francis of Assisi: A New Biography* (Ithaca: Cornell University Press, 2012).

3. Francis and His Spirituality

D. Flood and T. Matura, *The Birth of a Movement: A Study of the First Rule of St. Francis* (Chicago: Franciscan Herald Press, 1975; St. Bonaventure, NY: Franciscan Institute Publications, 2007).

E. Leclerc, *The Wisdom of the Poverello* (Chicago: Franciscan Herald Press, 1961).

T. Matura, *Francis of Assisi: The Message in His Writings* (St. Bonaventure: Franciscan Institute Publications, 2004).

C. Bobin, *The Very Lowly: A Meditation on Francis of Assisi* (Boston-London: New Seeds, 2006).

M. Bodo, *Francis: The Journey and the Dream* (Cincinnati: St. Anthony Messenger Press, 2011).

M. Bodo, *The Way of St. Francis* (Cincinnati: St. Anthony Messenger Press, 1995).

W. Hugo, *Studying the Life of Saint Francis of Assisi* (New York: New City Press, 2011).

Studies in Early Franciscan Sources, Vol. 1: *The Writings of Francis of Assisi: Letters and Prayers*, ed. M. Blastic, J. M. Hammond, J. A. W. Hellmann (St. Bonaventure, NY: Franciscan Institute Publications, 2011).

Studies in Early Franciscan Sources, Vol. 2: *The Writings of Francis of Assisi: Rules, Testament and Admonitions*, ed. M. Blastic, J. M. Hammond, J. A. W. Hellmann (St. Bonaventure, NY: Franciscan Institute Publications, 2011).

FURTHER READINGS

To really know Saint Francis, nothing can replace direct contact with the *Writings* he left us and with the remembrances of his first companions or his first biographers.

By way of an illustration of the principal themes dealt with in this volume, we are offering here a brief anthology of these primitive texts.

I. THE WRITINGS OF FRANCIS[156]

1. The Admonitions

Each year at Pentecost all the brothers came together for chapter. It was a time not only for adjusting existing legislation but for retreat as well, for a renewed contact with the ideal, for a new definition of objectives. Francis took advantage of this time to propose anew one or another aspect of gospel life in fraternity. These admonitions or exhortations have come to us in the form of summaries such as the following.

THAT NOBODY SHOULD BE PROUD, BUT SHOULD GLORY IN THE CROSS OF THE LORD

Consider, O human being, in what great excellence the Lord God has placed you, because He created and formed you to the image of His beloved Son according to the body, and to His likeness according to the spirit. And all creatures that are under heaven, each in its own way, serve, know, and obey their Creator better than you do. And even the demons did not crucify Him, but you together with them have crucified Him and are still crucifying Him by taking delight in vices and sins. In what, then, can you glory? Even if you were so clever and wise that you possessed all knowledge, and knew how to interpret all kinds of language and how to investigate in detail heavenly things, in none of these things can you glory. In fact, one demon has known about heavenly things

---

[156] This selection of writings of Francis has been translated by Jean-François Godet-Calogeras from the latest Latin critical edition prepared by Carlo Paolazzi, *Francisci Assisiensis Scripta,* Spicilegium Bonaventurianum, 36 (Grottaferrata: Editiones Collegii S. Bonaventurae, 2009).

and still knows more about those of earth than all human beings, although there may have been someone who received from the Lord a special knowledge of the highest wisdom. In like manner, even if you were more beautiful and richer than anybody, and even if you could work wonders, enough to put demons to flight, all these things are contrary to you, and nothing belongs to you, and in none of these things can you glory. But in this we can glory: in our infirmities, and in bearing every day the holy cross of our Lord Jesus Christ.

Admonition V

On poverty of spirit

Blessed are the poor in spirit, for theirs is the kingdom of heaven (Matt 5:3). There are many who devote themselves to prayers and offices, and inflict many abstinences and pains upon their bodies. But for a single word that seems to be an insult to their person, or for anything that would be taken away from them, they are immediately scandalized and upset. These people are not poor in spirit, because someone who is truly poor in spirit hates himself and loves those who strike him on the cheek.

Admonition XIV

2. Legislation

In 1209 Francis "had a text written down in a few and simple words" which the Pope approved. This text, the first draft of the Rule of the Friars Minor, was taken up again, enlarged, and perfected during the annual chapters held by the brothers.

That Early Rule represents an important stage in the evolution toward the final draft, the Later Rule, or the Rule of 1223, approved by the Church.

Chapter VI: On the Recourse of the Brothers to the Ministers; and that no Brother shall be called Prior

In whatever places the brothers are, if they cannot observe our life, they shall have recourse as soon as they can to their minister, making this known to him. The minister in turn shall endeavor to provide for them as he would want to be done for him if he were in a similar position. And no one shall be called prior, but in general all shall be called lesser brothers. And each shall wash the feet of the other.

Early Rule VI

CHAPTER VII: ON THE MANNER OF SERVING AND WORKING

All the brothers, in whatever places they may be among other people for serving or working, shall not be treasurers or managers, nor shall they be overseers in the houses of those they are serving, nor shall they accept any office which would generate scandal or be detrimental to their souls. But they shall be the lesser ones and subject to all who are in the same house.

And the brothers who know how to work shall work and exercise the same trade which they have learned, if it were not against the good health of their souls and it could be performed honestly. For the prophet says: *You shall eat the labors of your hands; you are blessed and it shall be well with you* (Psalm 127:2). And the Apostle says: *Who does not want to work shall not eat* (2 Thessalonians 3:10); and: *Everyone shall remain* in that trade and office *in which he has been called* (1 Corinthians 7:24). And for their work they can receive all things necessary except money. And when it would be necessary, they shall go for alms like the rest of the brothers. And they shall be allowed to have the tools and instruments needed for their trades.

All the brothers shall always endeavor to exert themselves in good works, because it is written: "Always do something good, that the devil may find you occupied" (St. Jerome). And again: "Idleness is an enemy of the soul" (Benedictine Rule 48:1). Hence servants of God must always be engaged in prayer or in some good occupation.

The brothers shall be careful, wherever they may be, in hermitages or in other places, not to appropriate any place to themselves or defend it against anyone. And whoever would come to them, friend or foe, thief or robber, shall be received with kindness. And wherever the brothers are and in whatever place they meet, they must respect one another with spirit and love, and honor one another without complaining. And they shall be careful not to appear outwardly as sad and gloomy hypocrites, but they shall show themselves joyful in the Lord, cheerful and becomingly gracious.

Early Rule VII

Chapter XXIII: Prayer and Thanksgiving

Almighty, most holy, most high and supreme God, Father holy and just, Lord King of heaven and earth, for Your own sake we give You thanks because through Your holy will and through Your only Son with the Holy Spirit You have created all things spiritual and corporal and, after making us in Your own image and likeness, You placed us in paradise. And we, through our own fault, we fell.

And we give You thanks because, as through Your Son You created us, so through Your true and holy love with which You loved us You made Him to be born as true God and true man of the the glorious, ever-virgin, most blessed, holy Mary, and You willed that by His cross and blood and death we captives be redeemed.

And we give You thanks because Your Son Himself will come again in the glory of His majesty to send the wicked who have not done penance and have not known You into eternal fire, and to say to all who have known You and adored You and served You in penance: "Come, you blessed of my Father, receive the kingdom which has been prepared for you from the beginning of the world."

And because all of us, wretches and sinners, are not worthy to name You, we humbly pray that our Lord Jesus Christ, Your beloved Son, in Whom You were well pleased, together with the Holy Spirit, the Paraclete, to give You thanks as it pleases You and Him for everything, He Who always suffices You for all, through Whom You have done such great things for us. Alleluia!

And for the sake of Your love, we humbly beg the glorious Mother, the most blessed Mary ever virgin, Blessed Michael,

Gabriel and Raphael, and all the choirs of the blessed spirits, seraphim, cherubim, thrones, dominations, principalities,
powers, virtues, angels, archangels, Blessed John the Baptist,
John the Evangelist, Peter, Paul, and the blessed patriarchs,
prophets, innocents, apostles, evangelists, disciples, martyrs,
confessors, virgins, the blessed Elijah and Henoch, and all
the saints who were, and will be and are, to give You thanks
for these things, as it pleases You, most high true God, eternal and living, with Your dearest Son, our Lord Jesus Christ,
and the Holy Spirit, the Paraclete, for ever and ever. Amen.
Alleluia!

And all those within the holy Catholic and Apostolic
Church who want to serve the Lord God, and all the eccle-
siastic orders: priests, deacons, subdeacons, acolytes, exor-
cists, lectors, porters, and all clerics, all religious men and all
religious women, all youths and children, the poor and the
needy, kings and princes, workers and farmers, servants and
masters, all virgins, continent and married women, all lay
people, men and women, all infants, adolescents, young and
old, healthy and sick, all little ones and great ones, and all
peoples, races, tribes and tongues, all nations and all people
all over the world, who are and will be, we humbly ask and
beseech, all we lesser brothers, useless servants, that we all
persevere in the true faith and in penance, because other-
wise no one can be saved.

Let us love with whole heart, with whole soul, with whole
mind, with whole strength and fortitude, with whole understanding, with all powers, with whole might, whole affection,
all feelings, all desires and wills, the Lord God Who has giv-
en and gives to all of us our whole body, our whole soul and
our whole life, Who has created us, redeemed us and by His
mercy alone will save us, Who did and does all good things
for us, miserable and wretched, putrid and foul, ungrateful
and evil ones.

Therefore, let us desire nothing else, let us want nothing
else, let nothing else please us and cause us delight but our
Creator, Redeemer and Savior, the only true God, Who is the
fullness of good, all good, whole good, the true and supreme

good, Who alone is good, merciful, gentle, delightful and sweet, Who alone is holy, just, true and upright, Who alone is kind, innocent, clean, from Whom and through Whom and in Whom is all pardon, all grace, all glory of all penitents, of all just ones, of all the blessed rejoicing together in heaven.

Therefore, let nothing impede us, nothing separate us, nothing come between us. Let all of us in every place, at every hour and every time, every day and continually, truly and humbly believe and hold in our heart and love, honor, adore, serve, praise and bless, glorify and superexalt, magnify and give thanks to the most high and supreme eternal God, Trinity and Unity, Father and Son and Holy Spirit, Creator of all, Savior of all who believe in Him and hope in Him and love Him, Who, without beginning and without end, is unchangeable, invisible, indescribable, ineffable, incomprehensible, unfathomable, blessed, praiseworthy, glorious, superexalted, sublime, most high, gentle, lovable, delightful, and totally desirable above all things for ever and ever. Amen.

Early Rule XXIII

Chapter III: On the Divine Office and Fasting; and the Manner the Brothers shall go into the World

The clerics shall do the Divine Office according to the order of the holy Roman Church, excepting the psalter; for that reason they may have breviaries. The lay, however, shall say twenty-four Our Fathers for Matins; for Lauds five; for Prime, Terce, Sext, and None, for each of these, seven; for Vespers twelve; for Compline seven. And they shall pray for the dead. And they shall fast from the feast of All Saints until the Nativity of the Lord. The holy Lent which goes on for forty continuous days after Epiphany, which the Lord consecrated with his holy fast, those who voluntarily fast, may they be blessed by the Lord; those who do not want to keep it will not be obliged. But they shall fast during the other Lent until the Resurrection of the Lord. At other times they shall not be bound to fast except on Fridays. During a time of obvious need, however, the brothers shall not be bound by corporal fast. I counsel, admonish and exhort my brothers in the Lord

Jesus Christ that, when they go through the world, they do not quarrel or argue or judge others; but they shall be meek, peaceful and modest, gentle and humble, speaking honestly to everyone, as is becoming. They shall not ride horseback unless they are forced by an obvious necessity or an infirmity. Into whatever house they enter, they shall first say: "Peace to this house!" And according to the holy Gospel, they shall be allowed to eat of whatever food is set before them.

Later Rule III

CHAPTER V: ON THE MANNER OF WORKING

Those brothers to whom the Lord has given the grace of working shall work faithfully and devotedly so that, once idleness, the enemy of the soul, excluded, they shall not extinguish the spirit of holy prayer and devotion to which all temporal things must contribute. In payment for their work they shall receive things necessary for the body, for themselves and their brothers, excepting coin or money, and they shall do this humbly as is becoming for servants of God and followers of most holy poverty.

Later Rule V

CHAPTER VI: THAT THE BROTHERS SHALL APPROPRIATE NOTHING; AND ON BEGGING FOR ALMS AND ON THE SICK BROTHERS

The brothers shall not appropriate anything for themselves, neither house, nor place, nor anything. And as pilgrims and strangers in this world, serving the Lord in poverty and humility, they shall go begging for alms with confidence, and they shall not be ashamed because, for our sakes, our Lord made Himself poor in this world. This is that sublime height of most high poverty which has made you, my dearest brothers, heirs and kings of the Kingdom of Heaven, made you poor in temporal things but raised you high in virtues. Let this be your portion which leads into the land of the living. Clinging totally to it, most beloved brothers, never seek to have anything else under heaven for the name of our Lord Jesus Christ. And wherever the brothers are and meet one another, they shall show to one another that they are from the same family. And each one shall confidently make known his need to the other, because if a mother loves and cares for her son born of her flesh, how much more diligently must someone love and care for his brother according to the Spirit! And if any of them falls sick, the other brothers must serve him as they would want to be served themselves.

Later Rule VI

CHAPTER X: ON THE ADMONITION AND CORRECTION OF THE BROTHERS

The brothers who are the ministers and servants of the other brothers shall visit and admonish their brothers, and humbly and charitably correct them, not commanding them anything that would be against their soul and our rule. The brothers who are subject, however, shall remember that, for God's sake, they have renounced their own wills. Therefore, I strictly command them to obey their ministers in everything they have promised the Lord to observe and which is not against their soul and our rule. And wherever the brothers are, those who would know and feel they cannot observe the rule according to its spirit, they can and shall have recourse to their ministers. The ministers, on their part, shall receive them charitably and kindly, and have such familiarity with them that these same brothers may speak and deal with them as masters with their servants, for so it must be that the ministers be the servants of all the brothers. Moreover, I admonish and exhort the brothers in the Lord Jesus Christ to beware of all pride, vainglory, envy, greed, cares and worries of this world, detraction and murmuring. And those who are illiterate shall not be anxious to learn, but they shall pay attention to what they must desire above all: to have the Spirit of the Lord and Its holy activity, to pray always to Him with a pure heart, and to have humility, patience in persecution and infirmity, and to love those who persecute us, rebuke us and argue with us, because the Lord says: *Love your enemies and pray for those who persecute and calumniate you* (Matthew 5:44). *Blessed are those who suffer persecution for the sake of justice, for theirs is the kingdom of heaven* (Matthew 5:10). *But he who perseveres to the end shall be saved* (Matthew 10:22).

Later Rule X

3. The Testament of Saint Francis

Written "to help the brothers better observe the rule," the Testament is the best light one can shed on the latter, to bring out the spirit that animates all of this legislation.

Written in the last weeks of the life of the saint (September-October 1226), an expression of his deepest longings, it is a priceless document for an understanding of his spirituality, in particular his love of Christ and submission to the Church.

The Lord gave me, brother Francis, to begin to do penance in this way: While I was in sin, it seemed excessively bitter to me to see lepers. And the Lord himself led me among them and I did mercy with them. And when I left them that which seemed bitter to me had been changed into sweetness of the spirit and the body; and afterward I lingered a little and left the world [of Assisi].

And the Lord gave me such faith in churches that I would simply pray and speak in this way: "We adore you, Lord Jesus Christ, and to all your churches throughout the world, and we bless you, for through your holy cross you have redeemed the world."

Afterward the Lord gave me and still gives me such faith in priests who live according to the form of the holy Roman Church because of their order, that if they were to persecute me, I would still have recourse to them. And if I possessed as much wisdom as Solomon had and I came upon pitiful priests of this world, I would not preach contrary to their will in the parishes in which they live. And I desire to fear, love, and honor them and all others as my lords. And I do not wish to consider sin in them because I discern the Son of God in them and they are my lords. And I act in this way since I see nothing corporally of the most high Son of God in this world except his most holy Body and Blood which they receive and which they alone minister to others. And these most holy mysteries I wish to have honored above all things and to be reverenced and to have them reserved in precious places. Wherever I come upon his most holy written words in unbecoming places, I desire to gather them up and I ask that they be collected and placed in a suitable place. And we should honor and respect all theologians and those who minister the most holy divine words as those who minister spirit and life to us.

And after the Lord gave me brothers, no one showed me what I should do, but the Most High himself revealed to me that I should live according to the form of the Holy Gospel. And I had it written down in a few words and simply and the Lord Pope confirmed it for me. And those who came to receive that life gave everything which they might have to the poor; and they were content with one tunic, patched inside and out, with a belt and breechers. And we had no desire for anything more. We said the Office, the clerics as other clerics did, the laics said the Our Father. And quite willingly we stayed in churches. And we were without learning, and subject to all. And I was working with my hands, and I want to work; and I firmly want all the other brothers to work in some work that is honest. Let those who do not know how to work learn, not out of any desire of receiving wages for their work, but to give example and to avoid idleness. And when we are not paid for our work, let us have recourse to the table of the Lord, begging alms from door to door. As salutation, the Lord revealed to me that we are to say: "The Lord give you peace!"

Let the brothers beware that they by no means receive churches or poor dwellings or anything which is built for them, unless it is in harmony with that holy poverty which we have promised in the Rule, and let them always be guests there as pilgrims and strangers. And I firmly command all of the brothers through obedience that, wherever they are, they should not be so bold as to seek any letter from the Roman Curia either personally or through an intermediary, neither for a church or for some other place or under the guise of preaching or even for the persecution of their bodies;

but wherever they have not been received, let them flee into another land to do penance with the blessing of God. And I firmly wish to obey the general minister of this fraternity and another guardian whom it might please him to give me. And I wish to be so captive in his hands that I cannot go anywhere or do anything beyond obedience and his will, for he is my lord. And although I may be simple and infirm, I wish nonetheless always to have a cleric who will celebrate the Office with me as it is contained in the Rule. And all the other brothers are bound to obey their guardians and to celebrate the Office according to the Rule. And if any are found who do not celebrate the Office according to the Rule and who wish to alter it in any way or who are not Catholics, let all the brothers be obliged through obedience that wherever they come upon such one they must bring him to the custodian who is nearest to that place where they have found him. And the custodian is strictly bound through obedience to guard him strongly as a prisoner day and night, so that he cannot be snatched from his hands until he can personally deliver him into the hands of his minister. And the minister is strictly bound through obedience to send him with brothers who shall guard him as a prisoner day and night until they deliver him before the Lord of Ostia who is the lord, protector, and corrector of the entire fraternity.

And let the brothers not say: This is another Rule; because this is a remembrance, an admonition, an exhortation, and my testament, which I, little brother Francis, prepare for all of you, my blessed brothers, so that we may observe in a better catholic manner the Rule which we have promised to the Lord. And the minister general and all other ministers and custodians are bound through obedience not to add to or subtract from these words. And let them always have this writing with them along with the Rule. And in all the chapters which they hold, when they read the Rule, let them also read these words. And I through obedience strictly command all my brothers, cleric and lay, not to place glosses on the Rule or on these words, saying: They are to be understood in this way. But as the Lord has granted me to speak and to write the Rule and these words simply and purely, so shall you understand them simply and without gloss, and observe them with their holy manner of working to the end.

And whoever shall have observed these things, may he be filled in heaven with the blessing of the most high Father and on earth with the blessing of his beloved Son with the most Holy Spirit the Paraclete and with all the powers of heaven and all the saints. And I, little brother Francis, your servant, inasmuch as I can, confirm for you this most holy blessing both within and without.

4. Letter to the Faithful

We possess many of the letters which Saint Francis wrote. The Letter to the Faithful was probably written in 1221-22. It is really a small handbook of Christian living. To facilitate the understanding of a text that is compact and at first sight somewhat intricate, we propose a few subtitles.

In the name of the Lord, Father and Son and Holy Spirit. Amen.

To all Christians, religious, clerics and laics, men and women, to all who dwell in the whole world, Brother Francis, their servant and subject, sends homage with respect, true peace from heaven and sincere charity in the Lord.

Since I am the servant of all, I am held to serve all and to administer the fragrant words of my Lord. Hence, as I take into consideration that because of infirmity and weakness I could not visit each one in person, I have decided to send you by the present letter and message the words of our Lord Jesus Christ, who is the Word of the Father, and the words of the Holy Spirit, which are spirit and life.

That Word of the Father, so worthy, so holy and so glorious, the most high Father, from heaven through his holy angel Gabriel, announced his coming in the womb of the holy and glorious Virgin Mary, from whose womb he received the real flesh of our human fragility. Though he was rich above all things, together with the most blessed Virgin his mother, he wanted himself to choose poverty in this world.

And near his passion he celebrated the Passover with his disciples. And taking bread he gave thanks and blessed and broke it, saying: "Take and eat together, this is my body." And taking the cup he said: "This is my blood of the new testament, which for you and for many will be shed for the forgiveness of sins." Then he prayed to his Father, saying: "Father, if it can be done, let this cup pass from me." And his sweat became like drops of blood running down to the ground. Yet he put his will in the will of the Father, saying: "Father, your will be done, not as I want, but as you do." Such was the will of the Father that His Son, blessed and glorious, whom he gave to us and who was born for us, would offer himself with his own blood as a sacrifice and a victim on the altar of the cross. He did not do it for himself, through whom all things were made, but for our sins, leaving us an example that we might follow in his footprints. And he wants that all of us be saved by him and that we receive him with our heart pure and our body chaste. Few however are those who would want to receive him and be saved by him, though his yoke is sweet and his burden light.

Those who do not want to taste how sweet is the Lord and who love the darkness more than the light, not wanting to fulfill God's commands, are doomed. About such people does the prophet say: "Doomed are those who deviate from your commands." But O how happy and blessed are those who love God and do as the Lord himself says in the Gospel: "You shall love the Lord your God with your whole heart and with you whole mind, and your neighbor as yourself."

Let us therefore love God and adore Him with a pure heart and a pure mind, because He Himself, asking this above all, said: "True adorers will adore the Father in spirit and in truth." For all who adore Him should adore him in the spirit of truth. And let us say praises and prayers to him day and night, saying: Our Father, who are in heaven, because we should always pray and not give up.

And so we must confess all our sins to a priest, and let us receive from him the body and blood of our Lord Jesus Christ, because he who does not eat his flesh and does not drink his blood cannot enter the kingdom of God. However, one should eat and drink worthily, because he who receives unworthily eats and drinks judgment on himself, without distinguishing the body of the Lord, that is, without realizing it. Furthermore, let us do worthy fruits of penance. And let us love our neighbors as ourselves. And if one does not want to love them as oneself, at least do them no evil, but do them good.

Those who have received the power to judge others shall exercise judgment with mercy, just as they themselves want to obtain mercy from the Lord. For judgment without mercy shall be theirs who have not done mercy. Let us then have charity and humility, and let us do almsgiving because alms wash the stains of sins from souls. For people lose all things which they leave in this world, but they carry with them the wages of the charity and of the almsgiving which they did, for which they will have from the Lord a reward and an appropriate remuneration.

Furthermore we must fast and abstain from vices and sins and excessive food and drink, and be Catholic. We must also visit churches frequently, and venerate and revere clerics, not so much for themselves, should they be sinners, but because of their office and the administration of the most holy body and blood of Christ, which they offer in sacrifice on the altar and receive and administer to others. And let all of us know for certain that no one can be saved except through the holy words and the blood of our Lord Jesus Christ, which clerics say, announce and minister. And they alone must minister, and not others. Yet religious especially, who have renounced the world, are held to do more and greater things, but not to dismiss these.

We must hate our bodies with vices and sins, because the Lord says in the Gospel: "All evils, vices and sins come from the heart." We must love our enemies and do good to those who hate us. We must observe the precepts and counsels of our Lord Jesus Christ. We must also deny ourselves and put our bodies under the yoke of service and holy obedience, as everyone has promised the Lord. And let no one be held in obedience to obey anyone where a wrong or a sin would be committed. But the one to whom obedience has been committed and who is taken for greater shall be as the lesser one and the servant of the other brothers. And he shall have and do to each of his brothers the mercy that he would want to be done to himself if he were in a similar situation. Nor shall he get angry against a brother because of the brother's wrong, but with all patience and humility he shall admonish him kindly and support him.

We must not be wise and prudent according to the flesh, but we must rather be simple, humble, and pure. And we shall hold our bodies in scorn and contempt, because all of us, through our fault, are lousy and stinking, rotten and worms, just as the Lord says through the prophet: "I am a worm and not a human, a scorn of human beings and the outcast of the people." We must never desire to be above others, but rather we must be servant and subject to all human creatures for God.

And all men and women who have done such things and persevered to the end, on them will rest the spirit of the Lord and in them make his home and dwelling. And they will be children of the heavenly Father whose works they do. And they are the spouses, the brothers and sisters, and the mothers of our Lord Jesus Christ. We are spouses when by the Holy Spirit the faithful soul is joined to Jesus Christ. We are his brothers and sisters when we do the will of his Father who is in heaven. We are mothers when we bear him in our heart and body through love and a pure and sincere conscience; and we give birth to him through a holy activity, which must shine in example to others.

O how glorious and holy and great it is to have a Father in heaven! O how holy, comforting, beautiful and admirable to have a spouse! O how holy and how beloved, well pleasing, humbling, peace-giving, sweet and lovable, and above all things desirable to have such a brother and such a son, who put down his soul for his sheep and prayed to the Father for us saying: "Holy Father, preserve in your name those whom you have given me. Father, all whom you have given me in the world, yours they were and you have given them to me. And the words you have given me, I have given them; and they have accepted them and know truly that I have come from you, and they have believed that you have sent me. I pray for them and not for the world; bless them and make them holy. And I make myself holy for them so that they may be made holy in being one as we too are. And I want, Father, that where I am, they also be with me, that they may see my brightness in your kingdom."

To him who underwent so many things for us, who has given us so many good things and will do so in the future, let every creature in heaven, on earth, in the sea and in the depths, give God praise, glory, honor and blessing, because He is our strength and courage, who alone is good, alone most high, alone allmighty, admirable, glorious and alone holy, praiseworthy and blessed for endless ages. Amen.

However, all those who are not in penance, and do not receive the body and blood of our Lord Jesus Christ, and are active in vices and sins, and who wander after bad concupiscence and bad desires, and do not observe what they have promised, and serve the world bodily by the carnal desires, by the cares and worries of this world, and by the cares of this life, deceived by the devil whose children they are and whose works they do, they are blind, because they do not see the true light, our Lord Jesus Christ. They do not have spiritual wisdom, for they do not have the Son of God in them, who is the true wisdom of the Father. About them it is said: "Their wisdom has been swallowed up." They see, they recognize, they know and they do bad things, and knowingly they lose their souls.

See, blind people, you are being deceived by our enemies, that is, by the flesh, by the world and by the devil, because it is sweet to the body to commit sin and bitter to serve God, because all evils, vices and sins come and proceed from the human heart, just as the Lord says in the Gospel. And you have nothing in this world and nothing in the future. You think to possess for a long while the vanities of this world, but you are deceived, because the day and hour will come of which you do not think and do not know and ignore.

The body becomes weak, death approaches, come relatives and friends saying: "Make a disposition of your things." Look, his wife and his children, and his relatives and friends make believe to weep! Looking back he sees them weeping and is moved the wrong way. Thinking to himself he says: "Look, I put in your hands my soul and body and all my things." Truly, this man is doomed who confides and entrusts his soul and body and all his things to such hands. That is why the Lord says through the prophet: "Doomed the human who trusts in human."

And immediately they make a priest come. The priest says to him: "Do you want to receive penance for all your sins?" He answers: "I want to." "Do you want to make satisfaction, as much as you can, out of your fortune, for what you have done and the ways you have defrauded and deceived people?" He answers: "No." And the priest says: "Why not?" "Because I have disposed of all my things in the hands of my relatives and friends." And he begins to lose his speech, and so does that miserable die of a bitter death.

But everyone shall know that wherever and however a human dies in criminal sin without satisfaction, when he could make make satisfaction and did not, the devil snatches his soul from his body with anguish and tribulation such as one cannot know if he does not get it. And all the talents and power and knowledge which he thought he had will be taken away from him. And he leaves his fortune to relatives and friends, and they will take and divide it and say afterwards: "Doomed be his soul, because he could have given us more and acquired more than he had acquired!" The worms eat the body, and so he loses body and soul in this brief world and will go to hell where he will be tortured without end.

All those this letter will reach, I, Brother Francis, your lesser servant, I ask and beseech you in the charity which God is, and with the will to kiss your feet, that you kindly receive and put into action and observe these words and the others of our Lord Jesus Christ, with humility and charity. And those who cannot read shall have these words read to them often, and they shall keep them with a holy activity to the end, because they are spirit and life. And those who will not do it, they shall render an account on the day of judgment before the tribunal of Christ. And all men and women who will receive them kindly, understand them and send copies of them to others, if they have persevered in them to the end, may the Father and the Son and the Holy Spirit bless them. Amen.

5. The Prayer of Saint Francis

Thomas of Celano has said that "Francis was no longer a man who prayed but prayer become man!" We still have many of the texts through which he expressed this prayer. Here are two of them.

At that time, walking in simplicity of spirit, they still ignored the ecclesiastical office. He said to them: "When you pray, say 'Our Father,' and 'We adore you, Christ, here and in all your churches which are in the whole world, and we bless you, because by your holy cross you have redeemed the world'."

Thomas of Celano, *Life of St. Francis*, 45

Almighty, eternal, just and merciful God, give us, miserable ones, to do, because of yourself, what we know you to want, and always to want what is pleasing You, that interiorly cleansed, interiorly enlightened and inflamed by the fire of the Holy Spirit, we may follow the footprints of Your beloved Son, our Lord Jesus Christ, and, by Your grace alone, make our way to You, Most High, Who in perfect Trinity and simple Unity live and reign and are glorified, God almighty, forever and ever. Amen.

Letter to the Entire Order 50-52

6. The Canticle of Brother Sun

Until the end – for it was almost on his deathbed that he composed his most joyful canticle – Saint Francis wanted to set the world in a state of praise.

During the fall of 1225, exhausted by the stigmatization and his sickness, he had withdrawn to San Damiano. Almost blind, alone in his reed hut, stricken by fever and tormented by field mice – out of all this sprang his song of love to the Father of all creation.

Most high, all-powerful, good Lord,
Yours are the praises, the glory, the honor, and all bless-
     ing.
To you alone, Most High, do they belong,
and no human is worthy to mention your name.
Praised be you, my Lord, with all your creatures,
especially Sir Brother Sun,
who is the day and through whom you give us light.
And he is beautiful and radiant with great splendor;
of you, Most High, he bears significance.
Praised be you, my Lord, through Sister Moon and the
     stars,
in the sky you formed them clear and precious and beau-
     tiful.
Praised be you, my Lord, through Brother Wind,
and through the air, cloudy and serene, and every kind of
     weather
through which you give sustenance to your creatures.
Praised be you, my Lord, through Sister Water,
which is very useful and humble and precious and chaste.
Praised be you, my Lord, through Brother Fire,
through whom you light the night
and he is beautiful and playful and robust and strong.

Praised be you, my Lord, through our Sister Mother
    Earth,
who sustains and governs us,
and who produces varied fruits with colored flowers and
    herbs.
Praised be you, my Lord, through those who give pardon
    for your love
and bear infirmity and tribulation.
Blessed are those who will endure them in peace
for by you, Most High, they shall be crowned.
Praised be you, my Lord, through our Sister Bodily Death,
from whom no living human can escape.
Woe to those who will die in mortal sin.
Blessed are those whom death will find in your most holy
    will,
for the second death shall do them no harm.
Praise and bless my Lord and give him thanks
and serve him with great humility.

Canticle of Brother Sun[157]

II. Deeds and Sayings

1. The Kissing of the Leper

One day, while he was praying enthusiastically to the
Lord, he received this response: "Francis, everything you
loved carnally and desired to have, you must despise and
hate, if you wish to know my will. Because once you begin
doing this, what before seemed delightful and sweet will be
unbearable and bitter; and what before made you shudder
will offer you great sweetness and enormous delight."
    He was overjoyed at this and was comforted by the Lord.
One day he was riding his horse near Assisi, when he met
a leper. And, even though he usually shuddered at lepers,
he made himself dismount, and gave him a coin, kissing his
hand as he did so. After he accepted a kiss of peace from him,
Francis remounted and continued on his way. He then began

---

[157] Translated from the Umbrian by Jean-François Godet-Calogeras.

to consider himself less and less, until, by God's grace, he came to complete victory over himself.

After a few days, he moved to a hospice of lepers, taking with him a large sum of money. Calling them all together, as he kissed the hand of each, he gave them alms. When he left there, what before had been bitter, that is, to see and touch lepers, was turned into sweetness. For, as he said, the sight of lepers was so bitter to him, that he refused not only to look at them, but even to approach their dwellings. If he happened to come near their houses or to see them, even though he was moved by piety to give them alms through an intermediary, he always turned away his face and held his nose. With the help of God's grace, he became such a servant and friend of the lepers, that, as he testified in his Testament, he stayed among them and served them with humility.

Legend of the Three Companions, 11[158]

2. Joy

The same [Brother Leonard] related in the same place that one day at Saint Mary of the Angels, blessed Francis called Brother Leo and said: "Brother Leo, write." And he responded: "Look, I'm ready!" "Write," he said, "what is true joy."

"A messenger arrives and says that all the masters of Paris have entered the Order. Write: this isn't true joy! Again, that all the prelates beyond the mountains, archbishops and bishops, and again, that the king of France and the king of England have entered. Write: this isn't true joy! Again, that my brothers have gone to the infidels and converted them all to the faith; again, that I have such a grace from God that I heal the sick and work many miracles. I tell you that in all these things there is not true."

"Then what is true joy?"

"I return from Perugia and arrive here in the depths of the night. It's winter time, muddy, and so cold that icicles form on the edges of my habit and keep striking my legs, and blood comes out of such wounds. And so all freezing, covered

---

[158] *FA:ED* 2, 74.

with mud and ice, I come to the door, and after I've knocked and called for quite a while, a brother comes and asks: 'Who are you?' I answer: 'Brother Francis.' And he says: 'Go away! This is not a decent hour to be going about! You may not come in!' And when I again insist, he would reply: 'Go away! You are a simpleton and an idiot! Don't come back to us again! We are so many and such that we do not need you!' And I stand again at the door and say: 'For the love of God, take me in tonight!' And he would reply: 'I will not! Go to the place of the Crosiers and ask there!' I tell you: If I had patience and did not become upset, in this is true joy and true virtue and the salvation of the soul."

The True Joy[159]

3. Simplicity and Discretion

One time in the very beginning, that is, at the time when blessed Francis began to have brothers, he was staying with them at Rivo Torto. One night, around midnight, when they were all asleep in their beds, one of the brothers cried out, saying: "I'm dying! I'm dying!" Startled and frightened all the brothers woke up. Getting up, blessed Francis said: "Brothers, get up and light a lamp." After the lamp was lit, blessed Francis said: "Who was it who said, 'I'm dying?'"

"I'm the one," the brother answered.

"What's the matter, brother?" blessed Francis said to him. 'Why are you dying?"

"I'm dying of hunger," he answered.

So that that brother would not be ashamed to eat alone, blessed Francis, a man of great charity and discernment, immediately had the table set and they all ate together with him. This brother, as well as the others, were newly converted to the Lord and afflicted their bodies excessively.

After the meal, blessed Francis said to the other brothers: "My brothers, I say that each of you must consider his own constitution, because, although one of you may be sustained with less food than another, I still do not want one who needs

---

[159] Translated by Jean-François Godet-Calogeras.

more food to try imitating him in this. Rather, considering his constitution, he should provide his body with what it needs. Just as we must beware of overindulgence in eating, which harms body and soul, so we must beware of excessive abstinence even more, because the Lord desires mercy and not sacrifice."

And he said: "Dearest brothers, great necessity and charity compelled me to do what I did, namely, that out of love for our brother we ate together with him, so he wouldn't be embarrassed to eat alone. But I tell you, in the future I do not wish to act this way because it wouldn't be religious or decent. Let each one provide his body with what it needs as our poverty will allow. This is what I wish and command you."

The first brothers and those who came after them for a long time mortified their bodies excessively, not only by abstinence in food and drink, but also in vigils, cold, and manual labor. Next to their skin, those who could get them wore iron rings and breastplates and the roughest hair shirts, which they were even better able to get. Considering that the brothers could get sick because of this, and in a short time some were already ailing, the holy father therefore commanded in one of the chapters that no brother wear anything next to the skin except the tunic.

We who were with him bear witness to this fact about him: from the time he began to have brothers, and also during his whole lifetime, he was discerning with the brothers, provided that in the matter of food and other things, they did not deviate at any time from the norm of the poverty and decency of our religion, which the early brothers observed. Nevertheless, even before he had brothers, from the beginning of his conversion and during his whole lifetime, he was severe with his own body, even though from the time of his youth he was a man of a frail and weak constitution, and when he was in the world he could not live without comforts.

One time, perceiving that the brothers had exceeded the norm of poverty and decency in food and in things, he said in a sermon he gave, speaking to a few brothers, who stood for all the brothers: "Don't the brothers think that my body needs special food? But because I must be the model and example for all the brothers, I want to use and be content with poor food and things, not fine ones."

The Assisi Compilation, 50[160]

One time when blessed Francis was at that same place, a certain brother, a spiritual man, an elder in religion, was staying there. He was very sick and weak. Considering him, blessed Francis was moved to piety toward him. The brothers back then, sick and healthy, with cheerfulness and patience took poverty for abundance. They did not take medicines in their illnesses, but more willingly did what was contrary to the body. Blessed Francis said to himself: "If that brother would eat some ripe grapes early in the morning, I believe it would help him."

One day, therefore, he secretly got up early in the morning, and called that brother and took him into the vineyard which is near that same church. He chose a vine that had grapes that were good and ready for eating. Sitting down with that brother next to the vine, he began to eat some grapes so that the brother would not be ashamed to eat alone, and while they were eating them, that brother praised the Lord God. As long as he lived, he always recalled among the brothers, with great devotion and flowing tears, the mercy the holy father had done to him.

The Assisi Compilation, 53[161]

4. Poverty

Blessed Francis gathered with the others in a place called Rivo Torto near the city of Assisi. In this place there was an abandoned hut. Under its cover lived these despisers of great and beautiful houses, protecting themselves from the torrents of rain. As the saint said, "It is easier to get to heaven from a hut than from a palace." All his sons and brothers were living in that same place with the blessed father, with great labor , and lacking everything. Often they

---

[160] *FA:ED* 2, 149-50.
[161] *FA:ED* 2, 152.

were deprived of the comfort of bread, content with turnips they begged in their need here and there on the plain of Assisi. The place in which they were staying was so narrow that they could barely sit or sleep in it.

Yet there was no complaining about this, no grumbling; but with peaceful heart, the soul filled with joy preserved the virtue of patience.

Saint Francis used to engage carefully in a daily, or rather, constant examination of himself and his followers. Allowing nothing dangerous to remain in them, he drove from their hearts any negligence. Unbending in his discipline, he was watchful of his guard at every hour. For if, as happens, any temptation of the flesh struck him, he would immerse himself in a ditch filled in winter with ice, remaining in it until every seduction of the flesh went away. The others avidly followed his example of mortifying the flesh.

Thomas of Celano, Life of St. Francis, 42[162]

He always strove for holy simplicity, refusing to allow the narrow place to restrict the breadth of his heart. For this reason, he would write the names of the brothers on the beams of that little house so that each would know his place when he wished to pray or rest, and the confines of the place would not disturb the silence of the spirit.

One day while they were staying there, a man came leading an ass to the little shelter where the man of God and his companions were staying. To avoid being sent away, the man urged the ass to enter by saying, "Get inside, for we shall do well for this place!" When the holy Francis heard this statement, he took it seriously, since he knew the man's intention: the man thought that the brothers wanted to stay there to expand the place by joining house to house. Immediately Saint Francis left the place, abandoning it because of what the peasant had said. He moved to another place, not far away, which was called "Portiuncula," where, as told above, he had repaired the church of Saint Mary a long time before.

---

[162] *FA:ED* 1, 220-21.

He wanted to own nothing so that he could possess every-thing more fully in the Lord.

Thomas of Celano, *Life of St. Francis,* 44[163]

Another time, in the place of Saint Mary of the Portiun-cula, the destitution was so great, that it was not possible to provide for the brothers coming as guests according to their needs. His vicar went to the man of God, pointing out the in-digence of the brothers and asking permission to save some of the goods of those entering as novices to which the broth-ers could have recourse in due season. Not ignorant of heav-enly guidance, the man of God said to him: "Far be it from us, dearest brother, to treat without piety what is in the Rule for the sake of anyone. I prefer that you strip the altar of the glorious Virgin, when necessity requires it, than to use some-thing or even a little that is contrary to the vow of poverty and the observance of the Gospel. For the Blessed Virgin will be happier to have her altar stripped and the counsel of the holy Gospel kept perfectly, than to have her altar decorated and her Son's counsel, as promised, neglected."

Bonaventure, *Major Legend of St. Francis,* 7:4[164]

5. Obedience

In order to make a profit in every possible way, and melt down all the present time into merit, this very shrewd busi-nessman chose to do everything under the harness of obedi-ence and to submit himself to the rule of another.

He not only resigned the office of general, but also, for the greater good of obedience, he asked for a special guardian to honor as his personal prelate. And so he said to Brother Peter of Catanio, to whom he had earlier promised obedience: "I beg you for God's sake to entrust me to one of my compan-ions, to take your place in my regard and I will obey him as devoutly as you. I know the fruit of obedience, and that no time passes without profit for one who bends his neck to the yoke of another." His request was granted, and until death

---

[163] *FA:ED* 1, 221-22.
[164] *FA:ED* 2, 579.

he remained a subject wherever he was, always submitting to his own guardian with reverence.

One time he said to his companions: "Among the many things which God's mercy has granted me, he has given me this grace, that I would readily obey a novice of one hour, if he were given to me as my guardian, as carefully as I would obey the oldest and most discerning. For a subject should not consider his prelate a human being, but rather the One for love of whom he is subject. And the more contemptibly he presides, the more pleasing is the humility of the one who obeys."

Another time, when he was sitting with his companions, blessed Francis let out a sigh: "There is hardly a single religious in the whole world who obeys his prelate perfectly!" His companions, disturbed, said to him: "Tell us, father, what is the perfect and highest obedience?" And he replied, describing someone truly obedient using the image of a dead body: "Take a lifeless corpse and place it wherever you want. You will see that it does not resist being moved, does not complain about the location, or protest if left. Sit it on a throne, and it will look down, not up; dress it in purple and it will look twice as pale. This," said he, "is someone who really obeys: he doesn't argue about why he's being moved; he doesn't care where he's placed; he doesn't pester you to transfer him. When he's raised to an office, he keeps his usual humility, and the more he's honored, the more he considers himself unworthy."

On another occasion, speaking about this same matter, he said that things granted because of a request were really "permissions," but things that are ordered and not requested he called "holy obediences." He said that both were good, but the latter was safer. But he believed that the best of all, in which flesh and blood had no part, was the one by which one goes "among the non-believers, by divine inspiration" either for the good of one's neighbor or from a desire for martyrdom. He considered this request very acceptable to God.

Thomas of Celano, *The Remembrance of the Desire of a Soul,* 151-152[165]

---

[165] *FA:ED* 2, 344-45.

6. Action or Contemplation

The truly faithful servant and minister of Christ, Francis, in order to do everything faithfully and perfectly, directed his efforts chiefly to the exercise of those virtues which, by the prodding of the sacred Spirit, he knew pleased his God more. In this matter it happened that he fell into a great struggle over a doubt which, after he returned from many days of prayer, he proposed for resolution to the brothers who were close to him.

"What do you think, brothers, what do you judge better? That I should spend my time in prayer, or that I should travel about preaching? I am a poor little man, simple and unskilled in speech; I have received a greater grace of prayer than of speaking. Also in prayer there seems to be a profit and an accumulation of graces, but in preaching a distribution of gifts already received from heaven.

"In prayer there is a purification of interior affections and a uniting to the one, true and supreme good with an invigorating of virtue; in preaching, there is a dust on our spiritual feet, distraction over many things and relaxation of discipline.

"Finally, in prayer we address God, listen to Him, and, as if living an angelic life, we associate with the angels. In preaching, it is necessary to practice great self-emptying for people and, by living humanly among them, to think, see, speak, and hear human things.

"But there is one thing to the contrary that seems to outweigh all these considerations before God, that is, the only begotten Son of God, who is the highest wisdom, came down from the bosom of the Father for the salvation of souls in order to instruct the world by His example and to speak the word of salvation to people, whom He would redeem by the price of His sacred blood, cleanse with its washing and sustain with its draught, holding back for Himself absolutely nothing that He could freely give for our salvation. And because we should do everything according to the pattern shown to us in Him as on the heights of the mountain, it seems more pleasing to God that I interrupt my quiet and go out to labor."

When he had mulled over these words for many days with his brothers, he could not perceive with certainty which of these he should choose as more acceptable to Christ. Although he understood extraordinary things through the spirit of prophecy, this question he could not resolve with clarity on his own.

But God's providence had a better plan, that the merit of preaching would be shown by a sign from heaven, thus preserving the humility of Christ's servant.

He was not ashamed to ask advice in small matters from those under him, true Lesser Brother that he was, though he had learned great things from the supreme Teacher. He was accustomed to search with special eagerness in what manner and in what way he could serve God more perfectly according to His good pleasure.

As long as he lived, this was his highest philosophy, this his highest desire: to ask from the wise and the simple, the perfect and the imperfect, the young and the old, how he could more effectively arrive at the summit of perfection.

Choosing, therefore, two of the brothers, he sent them to Brother Sylvester, who had seen the cross coming out from his mouth, and, at that time, spent his time in continuous prayer on the mountain above Assisi. He was to ask God to resolve his doubt over this matter, and to send him the answer in God's name. He also asked the holy virgin Clare to consult with the purest and simplest of the virgins living under her rule, and to pray herself with the other sisters in order to seek the Lord's will in this matter. Through a miraculous revelation of the Spirit, the venerable priest and the virgin dedicated to God came to the same conclusion: that it was the divine good will that the herald of Christ should preach.

When the two brothers returned and told him God's will as they had received it, he rose at once, girded himself and without the slightest delay took to the roads. He went with such fervor to carry out the divine command, just as he ran along so swiftly as if the hand of God were upon him, giving him new strength from heaven.

Bonaventure, *Major Legend of St. Francis*, 12: 1-2[166]

7. Prayer

He celebrated the canonical hours with no less awe than devotion. Although he was suffering from diseases of the eyes, stomach, spleen, and liver, he did not want to lean against a wall or partition when he was chanting the psalms. He always fulfilled his hours standing up straight and without a hood, without letting his eyes wander and without dropping syllables.

When he was travelling the world on foot, he always would stop walking in order to say the Hours, and when he was on horseback he would dismount to be on the ground. So, one day when he was returning from Rome and it was raining constantly, he got off his horse to say the Office, and, standing for quite a while, he became completely soaked. He would sometimes say: "If the body calmly eats its food, which along with itself will be food for worms, the soul should receive its food, which is its God, in great peace and tranquillity."

He thought he committed a serious offense if he was disturbed by empty imaginings while he was at prayer. When such a thing would happen, he did not fail to confess it and immediately make amends. He had made such a habit of this carefulness that he was rarely bothered by this kind of "flies."

One Lent he had been making a small cup, so as not to waste any spare time. But one day as he was devoutly saying terce, his eyes casually fell on the cup and he began to look at it, and he felt his inner self was being hindered in its devotion. He grieved that the cry of his heart to the divine ears had been interrupted, and when terce ended he said, so the brothers could hear: "Alas, that such a trifle had such power over me as to bend my soul to itself! I will sacrifice it to the Lord, whose sacrifice it had interrupted!" Saying this he grabbed the cup and burned it in the fire. "Let us be

---

[166] *FA:ED* 2, 622-24.

ashamed," he said, "to be seized by petty distractions when we are speaking with the Great King at the time of prayer."

Thomas of Celano, *The Remembrance of the Desire of a Soul*, 96-97[167]

---

[167] *FA:ED* 2, 311.

CHRONOLOGY OF SAINT FRANCIS OF ASSISI

DATE	EUROPE	CHURCH	MONASTICISM	CRUSADES	ARTS	ST. FRANCIS
1095				1st Crusade	St. Mark's (Venice)	
1099	BEAUVAIS	Pascal II	FONTEVRAULT CITEAUX	Jerusalem Taken Death of the Cid		
1100					MOISSAC (Cloister) Song of William of Orange	
1108	LAON Fairs of Champagne		St. Bernard enters CITEAUX			
1114			PONTIGNY			
1115			CLAIRVAUX			
1116	AMIENS		SAINT-GILLES-du-GARD			
1118		Gelasius II	KNIGHTS TEMPLAR			
1119		Callixtus II				
1120	CORBIE		PREMONTRE		Song of Roland VEZELAY, VERONA SAINT-FRONT, AUTUN	
1125		Honorius II			Pilgrimage of Charlemagne	
1127	SOISSONS, LILLE, BRUGES SAINT-OMER, BRESCIA	Sect of the Petrobrusians			Historia Hierosolymitana	

DATE	EUROPE	CHURCH	MONASTICISM	CRUSADES	ARTS	ST. FRANCIS
1130		Innocent II			FONTENAY, PARMA, PALERMO, SENS, CHARTRES Sculpt	
1143		Celestine II	TEUTONIC KNIGHTS		Marcabru	
1144		Lucius II				
1145		Eugene III				
1146	ROME*	Sect of the Lombards		2nd Crusade	Chanson des Chétifs Roman d'Alexandre ANGERS	
1152	VEZELAY*				NOYON,	
1153		Anastasius IV			SENLIS	
1154		Adrien IV				
1158			MILITARY ORDER of CALATRAVA		Raoul of Cambrai Bernard de Ventadour	
1159		Alexander II				
1160	ROUEN*				Tristan et Iseult Chretien de Troyes	
1163					NOTRE-DAME de Paris	
1166			MILITARY ORDER of ALCANTARA			
1167	Lombard League					
1169				Siege of Damietta		

CHRONOLOGY OF SAINT FRANCIS OF ASSISI

DATE	EUROPE	CHURCH	MONASTICISM	CRUSADES	ARTS	ST. FRANCIS
1171					TOURNAI	Birth of St. Dominic
1173		Waldensians in Lyons				
1175					SOISSONS Lais of Marie de France	
1179		3rd Lateran Council Condemnation of the Albigensians				
1181		Lucius III forbids Waldensians to preach				
1182				Crusade said to be "of the Capetians"		Birth of St. Francis
1185		Urban III			Palermo	
1187	Venetian trading posts in Byzantine Empire	Reconciliation of pope and commune of Rome Gregory VIII Clement III				
1188			Monastery of PATMOS	Conference of Gisors for 3rd Crusade	Glory portico at St. James of Compostella	
1190			The "Poor of Christ" (Later GRANDMONT)	3rd Crusade	BOURGES	
1191		Celestine III				

DATE	EUROPE	CHURCH	MONASTICISM	CRUSADES	ARTS	ST. FRANCIS
1192	Venice creates hard currency	Amalricians	Joachim of Fiora	Fall of Cyprus and Acre		
1198	New Italian trading posts in Byzantine Empire	Innocent III War against the Germans of Sicily	TRINITARIANS			
1199				Preaching of the 4th Crusade by Foulques de Neuilly		
1200	ASSISI				Perceval	
1201	GAUTHIER DE BRIENNE in South-ern Italy					
1202				4th Crusade Zara taken	Choir of ROUEN	PONT-SAINT-JEAN Captivity
1203		P. de CASTELNAU inquisitor		Sidon taken	Quest for the Holy Grail	Sickness
1206	Venetians occupy Crete	St. Dominic among the Albigensians			ROBERT OF CLARI *The Conquest of Constantinople*	SAN DAMIANO (conversion)
1208		Assassination of P. de CASTELNAU	ORDER of PREACHERS CARMELITES			GOSPEL at the PORTIUNCULA 1st Fraternity

CHRONOLOGY OF SAINT FRANCIS OF ASSISI

DATE	EUROPE	CHURCH	MONASTICISM	CRUSADES	ARTS	ST. FRANCIS
1210	Italian Communes: consuls replaced by podestas				VILLEHARDOUIN: On the Conquest of Constantinople	Confirmation of the Rule by the pope
1211					REIMS	
1212				Las Navas de Tolosa	MONT-SAINT-MICHEL	Departure for the Orient, then for Morocco.
1213			CHARITABLE ORDER OF THE HOLY SPIRIT			Stopover in Spain
1214	BOUVINES					
1215		4th Lateran Council				Meeting with St Dominic
1216		Honorius III		5th Crusade		
1217				Setback at Mt. Tabor	LE MANS	Trip to France interrupted
1218				JEAN DE BRI-ENNE in Egypt		Trip to Egypt and the Holy Land
1221		Death of St. Dominic		Loss of Damietta	AMIENS	Early Rule
1223			ORDER OF SERVITES			Later Rule Christmas in GRECCIO
1224						Stigmatization

DATE	EUROPE	CHURCH	MONASTICISM	CRUSADES	ARTS	ST. FRANCIS
1226	Louis IX, King of France				Lancelot in prose	Death of St. Francis
1227		Gregory IX				
1228						Canonization